GREAT CITIES

THROUGH THE AGES

PARIS

First American Edition published in 2003
by Enchanted Lion Books
115 West 18 Street, New York, NY 10011

LIBRARY OF CONGRESS CATALOGING-IN-PUBLICATION DATA
Rossi, Renzo, 1940-
Paris / Renzo Rossi — 1st American ed.
    p. cm — (Great cities through the ages)
    Includes index.
    Summary: Illustrations and text provide an overview of the history
of Paris, France. Contents: Early man from Lutetia to Paris — Paris
in the Middle Ages — Renaissance Paris — 17th century Paris —
Early architectural styles — Revolutionary times — Napoleon and
the restoration — Parisian street life — Meeting places — The
underground city — Parisian scenes — The glass and metal era —
The Second Empire — Haussmann's open spaces — The Belle
Epoque — The joy of living — Between the two wars — 1945 to the
present — Modern Paris.

    ISBN 1-59270-004-7

    1. Paris (France)—History—Juvenile literature. [1. Paris (France)—
History.]   I. Title. II. Series.
DC707.R655 2003
944'.361—dc21   2003040807

Printed and bound in Belgium
1 2 3 4 5 / 09 08 07 06 05 04 03

McRae Books Srl
Borgo S. Croce, 8, 50122 — Florence, Italy
info@mcraebooks.com

Text: Renzo Rossi
Illustrations: Andrea Ricciardi di Gaudesi, Studio Stalio (Alessandro
Cantucci, Fabiano Fabbrucci, Andrea Morandi, Ivan Stalio), Lorenzo
Cecchi, Lucia Mattioli, Antina Breithaupt, Gian Paolo Faleschini
Graphic Design: Marco Nardi
Layout: Sebastiano Ranchetti
Editors: Claire Moore, Anne McRae
Picture Research: Claire Moore, Loredana Agosta
Cutouts: Filippo Delle Monache, Alman Graphic Design
Translation: Claire Moore
Color Separations: Litocolor, Florence (Italy)

ACKNOWLEDGEMENTS
All efforts have been made to obtain and provide compensation for the
copyright to the photos and artworks in this book in accordance with
legal provisions. Persons who may nevertheless still have claims are
requested to contact the copyright owners.

t=top; tl=top left; tc=top center; tr=top right; c=center; cl=center left;
cr=center right; b= bottom; bl=bottom left; bc=bottom center; br=bottom right

The Publishers would like to thank the following museums and
institutions for their permission to publish their images.

10–11b © PMVP/Joffre; 11tr © PMVP/Svartz; 12b © PMVP/Svartz; 15b
© PMVP/Toumazet; 16–17b © PMVP/Ladet; 18–19b © PMVP/Joffre; 21tr
© PMVP/Berthier; 24t © PMVP/Abdourahim; 24b Marc Chagall "© The
Solomon R. Guggenheim Foundation, New York"; 24–25c © PMVP/Ladet;
26tr © L & M Services B.V. Amsterdam 20030110; 27t Photo Scala,
Florence; 28c "© Photo RMN" – J. L'hoir; 31t © PMVP/Andreani;
37tl © PMVP/Lifermann.

The Publishers would also like to thank the following photographers and
picture libraries for the photos used in this book.

Corbis/Contrasto: 14cl, 14b, 22tl, 40tr, 41tr, 41cr, 42tl, 42cl, 42cr;
Farabola Foto (The Bridgeman Art Library): 12tl, Archives Charmet
20–21b, 24–25t, 25cr, 25br, 27bc, 29c, Archives Charmet 30cr, 35tr,
37c, 39tr; Lonely Planet Images: 21cr Christine Osborne, 23tr Martin
Moos; Marco Nardi: 25bc, 30tl, 32tl; Rue des Archives: 14cr, 22–23c;
The Image Works: 21br, 27cr, 36cl, 41b.

GREAT CITIES THROUGH THE AGES

PARIS

Renzo Rossi

ENCHANTED LION BOOKS
New York

During medieval times, the Louvre became the residence of the king, Charles V. From an austere fortress, it was transformed into a fine palace.

This Roman pilaster, found under Notre-Dame in 1711, shows an ancient sailor of the Seine.

Table of Contents

Following the decision to develop the axis from the Etoile to the Défense, the Arch of the Défense was constructed. Exterior elevators whisk visitors to the panoramic rooftop.

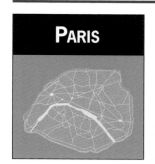

c. 4,500 BC Signs of settlement by the Seine.

c. 400 BC The Parisii tribe settle along the Seine.

200 AD The Arena, Forum, and Cluny Baths are constructed in Roman Lutetia.

c. 275 AD Lutetia is renamed Paris.

987 Hugh Capet is crowned king of France. Under the Capetian kings, Paris gains political stability and social order.

1348–49 The Black Death strikes in Paris.

1572 The St. Bartholomew's Day Massacre.

1643–1715 Louis XIV, the Sun King, reigns.

1789 The Storming of the Bastille on July 14.

1793 Louis XVI is guillotined in Place de la Concorde.

1793–94 The Reign of Terror.

1799 Napoleon Bonaparte takes power.

1830 The July Revolution.

1848 The Second Empire begins.

1870–71 Siege of Paris

leads to Paris Commune.

1889 The Eiffel Tower opens.

1940–44 German troops occupy Paris.

1968 Student uprisings.

1981–92 President Mitterrand begins a series of great architectural projects.

Introduction

One of the many Wallace Fountains found around Paris. Donated by Richard Wallace in the 19th century, they serve as drinking fountains.

Like many cities, Paris grew up at the crossroads of important land and water routes. By Roman times, in the 1st century BC, the original Celtic settlement on the Île-de-la-Cité had spread beyond the island in the Seine River. The decline of the Roman Empire in the 4th-6th centuries harmed Paris as much as the rest of Europe and the city only really recovered around 1000 when the Capetian kings provided sufficient political stability to stimulate both economic and population growth. Paris grew steadily through the later Middle Ages, despite frequent fires and recurrent bouts of plague. During the Renaissance the first efforts were made to plan the urban landscape and elegant squares appeared all over the city alongside imposing palaces with classical façades. French kings and aristocrats, together with an increasingly wealthy bourgeoisie, all sought to express their power and influence by erecting public buildings and monuments and constructing beautiful private homes. But it was only in the 19th century, when Napoleon III engaged Baron Haussmann to modernize the city, that Paris began to take on its current appearance with sweeping boulevards and streets lined with apartment houses in the classical style. Magnificently modern, Paris hosted several World Fairs and inaugurated its most recognizable landmark – the Eiffel Tower – during this time. For most of the 20th century Paris was a beacon for artists and writers, both from France and abroad, and it became the world capital of art and intellectual pursuits. The final decades of the 20th century were marked by large-scale urban renewal, culminating in Mitterrand's "grands projets," which has both respected the city's role as a European capital and underlined its character as an international trendsetter in terms of architecture and style.

The act of foundation of the original Sorbonne college. Founded in 1253 by the theology master, Robert de Sorbon, the Sorbonne University is now one of the world's leading universities.

Since the 17th century, Paris has been famous for its café society. The Procope is the oldest café in Paris. Opened in 1686, it welcomed clients such as Voltaire and Napoleon in its early years.

A flask from 300 AD found on the Île de la Cité.

The Parisii

The Parisii built wooden bridges to link their island to both banks of the Seine River. In this way they controlled the ford and the passage of boats up and down the river. Skilled sailors on both river and sea, the Parisii were able to dominate the valuable trading of British tin, which brought them great economic prosperity.

In the 1st century AD the arena in Lutetia (reconstruction below) was used for shows and gladiator fights.

A gold coin of the Parisii tribe.

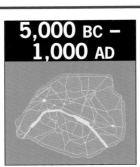

5,000 BC – 1,000 AD

c. 5,000 BC Agriculture begins on Île-de-France.

1,800–750 BC The Seine River becomes an important route for commercial trade.

c. 400 BC A Celtic tribe — the Parisii — found the fortified town of Lutetia.

From Lutetia to Paris

Lutetia Parisiorum

The Roman city, Lutetia Parisiorum, extended over 133 acres of land: 22 acres on the Île de la Cité where the governor's headquarters and the temple were built, and 111 acres on the Left Bank of the Seine. With around 8,000 inhabitants, Lutetia Parisiorum had all the usual public buildings of a Roman city. In addition to the forum, there was a courthouse, a porticoed square, three bathhouses fed by a 10-mile-long aqueduct, a theater, and an amphitheater which, with 15,000 seats, was the largest in Gaul. A temple dedicated to Mercury stood on the Right Bank.

In 200 BC, the streets of Lutetia were laid out in a geometric pattern, following the model of a classic Roman city.

Île de la Cité

Temple

Cluny Baths

Theater

Seine River

Forum

Southern Baths

Baths of the College of France

Main street

Arena

T he Paris area shows traces of human settlement from about 700,000 years ago. For thousands of years after that it was inhabited by bands of nomadic hunters and gatherers. In Neolithic times, around 5,000 BC, small groups of people from the Danube Valley began to move into the area, introducing the use of pottery and settled farming. In the 5th century BC, the Celts arrived and one of their tribes, the Parisii, settled along the Seine River. They built the fortified village of Lutetia (Latin for "midwater-dwelling") on the island in the river now known as the Île de la Cité. Julius Caesar began his conquest of Gaul (as France was known in Celtic times) in 58 BC, and Lutetia fell into the hands of his general, Labienus. Three centuries later Lutetia took the name of Paris.

Lutetia becomes Paris

Under the Romans, Lutetia remained a city of little importance, never reaching, in contrast to Lyons, the status of provincial capital. From the middle of the 3rd century, however, it began to assume an important military role in the defense of the northern and eastern borders of Gaul from Germanic invasion. At this time it was renamed Paris, an abbreviation of Parisiorum.

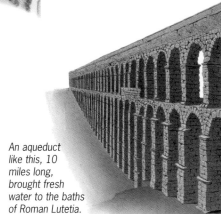

An aqueduct like this, 10 miles long, brought fresh water to the baths of Roman Lutetia.

52 BC Lutetia is conquered by the Romans.

c. 250 AD Martyrdom of Saint Denis, the first bishop of Lutetia.

c. 275 First Germanic invasions. Lutetia takes the name of Paris.

451 Attila the Hun threatens

Paris. A girl called Geneviève exhorts Parisians to hold their ground and pray. Attila and his army avoid Paris. Geneviève later becomes patron saint of the city.

486 Clovis, king of the Franks, seizes Paris and founds the Merovingian dynasty.

496 Clovis and the Franks convert to Catholicism.

508 Clovis makes Paris the capital of his kingdom.

511 Childebert, son of Clovis, becomes king of Paris.

561 The kingdom of the Franks is divided into three

parts; Paris is the capital of Neustria (between Schelda and the Loire).

754 Pippin the Short is consecrated in the church of Saint-Denis. The Carolingian dynasty begins.

845 Viking invasions of Paris begin.

855 Paris is sacked and destroyed by the Vikings. The Cité resists the order of Bishop Oddone.

987 Hugh Capet is crowned king of France. Paris becomes his capital. The Capet dynasty begins.

Alaric II, king of the Visigoths, pays homage to Clovis I (seated on his horse), after being defeated by him at the Battle of Campus Vogladensis in 507.

Invasion of the Franks

During the 5th century, Germanic Franks from the Rhine continued to invade France under their ruler, Clovis I. They defeated the Gallo-Roman general Syagrius, who controlled the area between the Seine and the Loire, and in 486 occupied Paris, making it their capital. Clovis made France his kingdom and founded the Merovingian dynasty (the name derives from Merovech, founder of the family).

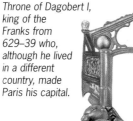
Throne of Dagobert I, king of the Franks from 629–39 who, although he lived in a different country, made Paris his capital.

The Merovingians and the Carolingians

When Clovis I died in 511 his kingdom was divided among his four sons, with Childebert becoming king of Paris. He built the Cathedral of Saint-Étienne on the Île de la Cité, and other important buildings soon followed, including the Royal Palace, the Archbishop's palace, the prison, and the mint. When the Carolingians came to power in the 8th century, they moved the center of Frankish power eastward, greatly reducing the importance of Paris.

The Vikings Lay Siege

By the end of the 9th century, the Vikings had attacked Paris on several occasions. Bands of Vikings plundered churches and monasteries, destroying what they could not pillage. In 885, 3,000 Danish Vikings laid siege to Paris,

The Viking siege of Paris in 885. The invasion of the Seine by Viking longboats began as early as 845.

leaving areas of the Right Bank of the city in ruins. Only the central island (la Cité), under Odo, count of Paris, successfully withstood the attack. For a time the city consisted of just the walled island, and when reconstruction did begin most of the new buildings arose on the Right Bank, which was better suited to river trade and had flat terrain that allowed the construction of a protective city wall.

The legendary Saint Denis carrying his own head.

Christianity

Christianity spread to Paris toward the middle of the 3rd century. The first bishop of the city was Saint Denis, who was decapitated by the Romans on a hill in Montmartre. A French legend claims that after he was killed, the saint's living body collected its own head and walked to his burial site, where today the Abbey of Saint-Denis stands.

The Capetian kings

In July 987 a powerful Parisian count called Hugh Capet was crowned king of France. This marked the beginning of the Capetian dynasty which remained in power until 1328. Under the Capetians, Paris was once more capital of France and the city gained in both prosperity and stability. A representative of the king, called the provost of Paris, was appointed to maintain law and order.

An 18th-century image of Hugh Capet.

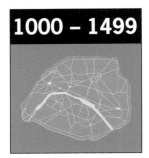

1060 Revival of country villages around Paris.

1190–1210 Construction of the city walls by Philippe-Auguste and of the Louvre.

1215 Founding of the University of Paris.

1226 Louis IX, Saint

Louis, ascends the throne.

1269 A municipal council of 24 merchants is founded. A bad flood destroys all the city's bridges.

Seal of the University of Paris.

1302 Founding of the Estates-General, an early form of French Parliament.

1313 Construction of the first embankment by the Seine River.

1339–1453 Hundred Years' War against England.

1348 The plague or "Black Death" strikes.

1364–80 Charles V enlarges the city walls on the Right Bank.

1420–36 During the Hundred Years' War the English occupy Paris. Period of Joan of Arc.

1461 Louis XI becomes king.

Fires – A Parisian Nightmare

Space was limited within the walls of medieval Paris and so houses were built one on top of the other, often growing in height, floor by floor. The upper floors were built jutting out above the lower ones, so much so that the houses on opposite sides of a street almost touched. The outer walls, if not of solid wood, were built of exposed wooden beams with the spaces filled with a mixture of clay and straw or, later, by stones or bricks. (A couple of these houses, reinforced in 1967, are still standing (Rue François Miron 11-13, IV arrondissement). This led to the recurrent nightmare of fires, which in just a few hours could raze entire city districts. Special officers were employed by the town council to prevent fires from breaking out in the first place.

Homes were heated by coal-burning braziers or open fires in the middle of a room. By the 13th century, wealthy homes had stone fireplaces built into the walls, like this one.

Paris in the Middle Ages

Paris was an important political and cultural center during the Middle Ages. The royal family moved into its palace on the Île de la Cité, not far from Notre-Dame Cathedral. By the 13th century, the maze-like city center had been enclosed by a three-mile-long wall. It also had its own university, famous throughout Europe for its school of theology. By 1300, Paris had 200,000 inhabitants and was governed by a council of wealthy middle-class men, against whom there were frequent revolts and popular uprisings. Relations between the king and Parisians were often stormy due to frequent famines, outbreaks of plague, and the war with England, which lasted, on and off, for more than 100 years.

Most homes had just a few simple pieces of furniture. However, a married couple's bed was often quite elaborate. It was made of solid wooden beams with a baldachin and curtains to keep out the drafts. The mattress was made of straw or, more rarely, of down, while the sheets were cut from whitened linen. The blankets were in wool or down. People slept in the nude although they sometimes wore a turban.

A Parisian market scene of the 1400s.

Keeping Clean

Medieval Paris, like most cities at the time, was smelly and filthy. It was not unknown for rats to attack children in their cribs! Butchers, tanners, dyers, and tripe-makers all worked in and around the crossroads at Grand Châtelet, where they poured the dirty water from their trades into the canals which flowed into the Seine River. Private citizens were no better, and they tossed trash out their windows, including the contents of chamber pots. In this case though, they were required to shout "watch out for the water!" Many houses had rudimentary outside toilets (left), but baths were a luxury that only the very wealthy could afford.

Feeding the City

At the turn of the 13th century, before the plague of 1348 decimated the city, Paris was the largest town in Europe. Hundreds of tons of grain and barrels of wine and beer were consumed every day. Huge numbers of cattle, pigs, and sheep were butchered, and vast quantities of fish, cheese, and salt were sold in the markets at Place de Grève and Champeaux (now Forum des Halles). Every morning at dawn a stream of carts laden with fruit and vegetables poured through the city gates. Many activities were concentrated in the area around the Grand Châtelet, where the names of the streets, such as La Grande Boucherie (the butcher shop), indicated the type of shops which could be found.

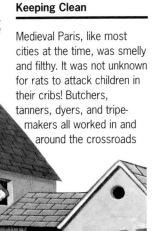

Clothing became more elaborate as the Crusaders brought back cotton, muslin, and gauze from the East. Married women (right), who had to cover their hair, usually wore a simple piece of white cloth turban-fashion, which fell over their faces. In the 15th century, among upper-class women (left), corn- and miter-shaped hats with light gauze veils came into fashion.

1469 The first French printing press begins operation at the Sorbonne.

1483 Charles VIII becomes king.

1498 Louis XII becomes king.

Street Life

The streets of Paris, especially those on the Île de la Cité, were always bustling, since so much of life took place outdoors. Workshops were situated on the ground floor of many houses and opened into the street, while itinerant salespeople set up their stalls all over the place. The passing crowd also harbored pickpockets, acrobats who performed in the churchyard of Notre-Dame, monks, and beggars, often pushed out of the way by the retainers of one lord or another who proceeded arrogantly along on horseback toward the royal palace. Hens, geese, and pigs wandered freely, scratching around in public fountains which served as drinking-troughs, or in the gutter that ran down the center of the street.

Paris was a thieves' paradise. Many wealthy homes had armed guards, but other middle-class homes were only protected by solid doors and locks (left). Moneychangers and goldsmiths used strong iron locks on their chests, turning them into safes.

The streets of Paris were completely dark at night, except for the weak light from the lamps in the occasional street shrine. Nightwatchmen patrolled the city with flickering lanterns and whoever was found to be out without good reason was arrested. University students fought among themselves to knock the watchmens' lanterns from their grip (by throwing stones) so that they would not be discovered out of their dormitories.

The Renaissance period in Paris was a time of rapid growth, both in terms of population and cityscape. The city emerged from the Hundred Years' War under the Valois kings as the capital of a territorially larger and militarily more secure nation. During the 16th century power was increasingly concentrated in the Valois kings at the expense of feudal lords and the city burgeoned accordingly. Ideas from the Italian Renaissance percolated north, becoming apparent in the reconstruction of the Notre-Dame Bridge and the Louvre and the inauguration of exciting new urban structures, such as the Hôtel de Ville, the Pont-Neuf Bridge, and the Tuileries Palace and gardens. From the mid-16th century France was torn by the Religious Wars between Roman Catholics and Protestant Huguenots and Paris was a frequent battleground.

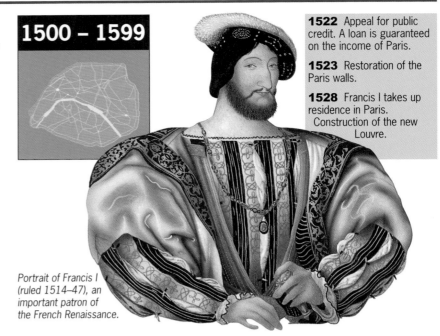

1500 – 1599

1522 Appeal for public credit. A loan is guaranteed on the income of Paris.

1523 Restoration of the Paris walls.

1528 Francis I takes up residence in Paris. Construction of the new Louvre.

Portrait of Francis I (ruled 1514–47), an important patron of the French Renaissance.

Renaissance Paris

The Church of Saint-Jacques de la Boucherie (in the butcher's quarter) was built at the beginning of the 16th century, as Italian Renaissance ideas began to influence architecture in Paris. This church, a favorite stopping place for pilgrims on their way to the sanctuary of Santiago de Compostela in Spain, was demolished in 1797. Today only the tower (left) remains.

Built by Pierre Lescot, this is the oldest surviving part of the Louvre. It was begun in 1546 during the reign of Francis I.

The Renaissance of the Louvre

In medieval times, the Louvre was a fortress dominated by a central keep that defended the Right Bank of the city. In 1358 Charles V transformed it into an elegant Gothic building, making it his official residence and a place of entertainment for the sovereign (gentlemen challenged each other to horse races along the corridors), but succeeding generations did not like the palace and it fell into ruin. In 1515 Francis I also made it his official residence and entrusted its renovation to Pierre Lescot, who rebuilt the palace in a classic style, while the famous sculptor Jean Goujon worked on the internal decoration. Henri II and his wife Catherine de Medicis extended the Louvre, adding the Hall of the Caryatids and the Grand-Degré staircase (now the Henri II staircase).

Regattas at the Notre-Dame Bridge

When the Notre-Dame Bridge, the most important bridge over the Seine, collapsed for the second time in 1499, city officials imposed a special tax on fish, livestock, and salt in order to rebuild it. Parisians did not grumble too much since public spectacles, watersports, regattas, and naval battles often took place at the bridge. Onlookers leaned out of the windows of the bridge's 68 houses, some six-storeys tall, or clung to the watermills that used the river's current to grind grain.

Hôtel de Ville

Few streets in the 16th century were more than 16 feet (5 m) wide. The architectural beauty of the new Renaissance buildings, however, needed more space. Place de Grève, one of the most important meeting places in medieval Paris, was the biggest open space in the city, and it was here, between 1532 and 1549, that Francis I built the Hôtel de Ville, Paris's city hall. Designed by Domenico da Cortona, who was known as Le Boccador, the building was destroyed in a fire in 1871. The building which stands there today was built in the 19th century.

The Seine from Pont Neuf

Begun in 1577 during the reign of Henri III, Pont Neuf was left unfinished until 20 years later when Henri IV completed it. It finally was opened in 1610. Built of solid stone, it was the longest and widest bridge in Paris at that time. It was also the first bridge to be built without houses and offered a fabulous view of the river. It succeeded in establishing a new rapport between the Cité and the river, and between medieval and Renaissance Paris. The Parisians were enthusiastic about the new bridge, and it soon became a popular venue for afternoon strolls and carriage rides.

1533 The dauphin, Henri of Orleans marries Catherine de Medicis of Florence, Italy.

1547 Francis I dies and is succeeded by Henri II.

1558 Large lamps to light crossroads are proposed in the city.

1560 Henri II dies in a tournament. Catherine de Medicis becomes regent for her son Charles IX.

1566 The church of Saint-Eustache is built.

1572 Protestants are massacred on the night of St. Bartholomew.

1574 Another son of Catherine de Medicis, Henri III, takes the throne.

1578 Henri III orders the construction of Pont Neuf.

1590 Under siege, Paris is contested between Henri III's troops and those of the future Henri IV.

1594 Henri IV enters Paris.

1596 Actors are admitted to the fairs at Saint-Germain and Saint-Laurent.

1598 With the Edict of Nantes, Henri IV concedes religious freedom to the Protestants.

Work started on the Notre-Dame bridge in 1507. 34 houses were built on each side, creating a straight thoroughfare.

The Wars of Religion (1562–98)

A bitter civil war took place in France between Roman Catholics and French Protestants, who were known as the Huguenots. Although religion was an important factor, the wars were also about politics and power. A key player in the struggle was the Queen regent — Catherine de Medicis, mother of the king, who was too young to rule. Catherine was a Catholic but she wanted to diminish the power of some noble Catholic families and so allowed the Huguenots to worship openly. The Catholics were enraged and attacked the Protestant worshipers who retaliated. The worst incidents in Paris were the St. Bartholomew's Day Massacre in August 1572, when thousands of Huguenots were hunted down and killed, and the Day of the Barricades (1588), when the Catholic League rose against Henri III. The wars ended in 1598, under Henri IV, when the Edict of Nantes extended religious freedom to the Huguenots.

A contemporary painting showing the massacre of the Huguenots on the night of St. Bartholomew. The French Protestants took the name Huguenots from the German term "Eidgenossen" meaning confederate.

The Pont-Neuf was a busy place, bustling with the activity of daily life.

The statue of Henri IV on Pont Neuf was the work of Giambologna and Pietro Tacca.

Court Fashion

The Queen, Catherine, in her black widow's clothes was not an influence on the fashions of her times, even though she wore some of the best pearls of the era. Italian styles, however, did make an impression on the men and women of the royal court. Cloth embellished with gold and silver embroidery, large linen ruff ties, and huge cloaks of silk and fur were all popular among the nobility. Men wore padded doublets, tights, or breeches, while women's gowns were voluminous with sleeves that puffed out and almost touched the floor. In the streets around the Louvre, there were many tailors, glovemakers, and perfumeries which supplied the noble clientele, both men and women, with ointments and powders to whiten their faces and hands, to redden their cheeks and lips, and to emphasize their eyes.

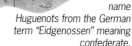

A Parisian noble couple at the end of the 16th century in their court finery.

An illustration of a young Catherine de Medicis. After the premature death of Henri II, she dressed in black for the rest of her life.

Peace Returns

The age of Henri IV saw the return of religious peace and was one of the most productive for the city. The king desired a powerful capital that would develop a new national conscience, and initiated new urban plans on simple, elegant lines. A gallery, linking the Louvre to the Tuileries, was the first of his projects, followed by Place Dauphine on the tip of Île de la Cité, Place Royale, which became a favorite place for festivals and exhibitions, and the hospital of Saint-Louis.

Louis XIV (above), succeeded to the throne in 1643 at the age of four. His youth was marred by a long civil war known as the Fronde (1648–74) during which a group of Parisian nobles tried to oust the monarchy. The young king suffered greatly and when he finally took real power in 1661 he neither trusted nor forgave either Paris or the nobles.

The Château of Versailles

Louis XIII built a hunting lodge at Versailles in 1623, enlarging it a few years later. From the 1660s his son, Louis XIV (the Sun King), employed more than 30,000 men over 20 years to extend the lodge and gardens, making it into one of the largest and most ornate castles in Europe. In 1682 the king moved his court to Versailles. Construction work continued with the Hall of Mirrors (symbolizing the power of the Sun King), the Orangery, the Stables, and the Royal Chapel.

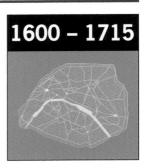

1600 – 1715

Paris in the 17th Century

Paris in the 17th century was marked by the personalities of two men — Cardinal Richelieu and Louis XIV. The first strengthened the power of the crown and played a decisive role in European politics. The second became famous, among other things, for his statement "*L'état, c'est moi*" (I am the state) and ruled over every minute detail of his kingdom. By force of arms, Louis XIV made France into the most powerful country in Europe. He was known as Louis the Great or The Sun King.

The Place Royale (below), which Napoleon later re-baptized the Place des Vosges, was inaugurated on April 5, 1612 with a magnificent festival to celebrate the marriage of Louis XIII and the Spanish Infanta, Anne of Austria. Initially a center for silk manufacture, under Louis XIII it developed into an important center of aristocratic and fashionable life.

1610 Assassination of Henri IV. Louis XIII succeeds under the regency (until 1617) of his mother, Maria de Medicis.

1624 Cardinal Richelieu becomes chief minister.

1626–42 Richelieu rebuilds the Sorbonne.

1635 Richelieu founds the Académie Française.

1643 Death of Louis XIII. Louis XIV succeeds under the regency of his mother, Anne of Austria. The court leaves the Louvre for the Palais-Royal.

1648 Cardinal Mazarin takes power.

1656 Workshops are banned from bridges.

1661 Louis XIV succeeds to the throne, following the regency period.

1665 Colbert becomes financial controller.

1667 Street lighting with candles positioned in metal lanterns is introduced.

1670 Demolition of the wall built by Charles V and Louis XIII.

1676 Boulevards begin to appear around Paris.

1680 Founding of the Comédie Française.

1682 Louis XIV transfers his court to Versailles.

1685 Revoke of the Edict of Nantes.

1702 Paris is divided into 20 quarters.

1715 The Sun King dies.

Many pedlars like this sold their knick-knacks on the streets of Paris.

The Poor Become Poorer

Huge amounts of money were required to create the splendor of Versailles, and Parisians became ever poorer as more and more taxes and duties were imposed. Many lived in poverty, packed into tiny houses in the center of the city, surviving on meager rations of bread, cheese, and fish. The streets were full of pickpockets, beggars, vendors hawking their wares, and those desperately seeking work. Although it was easier to find a way of supporting oneself in the suburbs and countryside, life was little better.

Continued Growth

Even after the king withdrew to Versailles, Paris continued to grow. Most of the new splendors were designed by the king's superintendent of finance, Jean-Baptiste Colbert. The tree-lined avenues of the Champs-Elysées were laid out in 1667 and the Tuileries Palace sumptuously redecorated. By 1700 Paris had 20,000 houses and almost 600,000 inhabitants, and was the largest city in Europe.

From 1686 rich Parisians could meet in the Procope, a café opened by the Sicilian Francesco Procopio. Sumptuously decorated with mirrors, chandeliers, and gilded ceilings, it served the fashionable drink of the times — hot chocolate.

Hôtel des Invalides — A Hospital for Old Soldiers

Soldiers no longer in active service, whether wounded or old, who otherwise risked a life of beggary or crime, were housed in the Hôtel des Invalides (above), built by Louis XIV in 1671. This immense complex with its austere façade was developed around a series of military courtyards, which encircled the church of Saint-Louis-des-Invalides. The pensioners, as they were called, were subject to a life of rigorous daily discipline.

Place des Victoires

No new piazzas had been built in Paris since the reign of Henri IV. But in the 1680s the idea of celebrating Louis XIV's military victories led to new piazzas being built all over France with a statue of the king at their center. In 1681 the Duke of La Feuillade, one of the king's courtiers, demolished two buildings near the Palais-Royal to build such a piazza in Paris. The architect Jules Hardouin-Mansart designed the circular piazza (above), 127 feet (39 m) in diameter and encircled by buildings with perfectly proportioned façades.

Below: Wealthier Parisians flocked to the theaters to see plays by Molière, Racine, and Corneille, and attended painting and sculpture exhibitions in the Louvre. This illustration shows French and Italian actors in the Théâtre Royal in 1670.

The Nain brothers worked in Paris in the middle of the 17th century. They illustrated the daily life of the poor in a series of paintings. This illustration shows peasant farmers in the countryside around Paris.

Entertainment

Even the poorest citizens had many chances to enjoy themselves in 17th century Paris. There were huge firework displays on the Pont Neuf for the Feast of St. John, the fairs of Saint-Denis (which lasted 2 months) and Saint-Germain to be enjoyed, and countless other parish festivals. For the rich, there were theaters, cabarets, and inns serving fine food. On fine days they drove their carriages along the Siene, eyeing each other's fine clothing, make-up, and wigs.

Elegant wooden furniture decorated with mother-of-pearl adorned the houses of the rich in 17th century Paris. The royal cabinetmaker Charles Boulle made furniture for Versailles.

Gothic architecture, the style of kings, lords, great monasteries, and the emerging bourgeoisie originated on the Île de France in the first half of the 12th century and dominated monumental French architecture until the beginning of the 16th century. In the 17th century, the Baroque style took over, although the French quickly adapted it to the discipline and ordered ideas of Classicism. At the beginning of the 18th century, however, this was replaced by a new graceful, sensual style — Rococo.

One of the grotesque gargoyles of the Chimere Gallery, which stands between the two towers of Notre-Dame. In Gothic art, architecture and sculpture are closely bound together.

ARCHITECTURE

1120 The first basilica of Notre-Dame is completed on the ruins of a Roman temple.

1220 The façade of Notre-Dame, apart from the towers, is finished.

c. 1230 The Gothic style of the Île de France spreads all over the kingdom.

1243 Building starts on Sainte-Chapelle.

1370 The first stone is laid at the Bastille.

1546 Work starts on the Cour Carrée (Square Courtyard) of the Louvre.

1645 Work on Val-de-Grâce military hospital begins.

1671 Foundation of the Academy of Architecture.

Right: A stained-glass window from Sainte-Chapelle shows a king being crowned. Large stained-glass windows were essential elements of the 14th century Gothic style. The light acted as a filter and allowed the image to be "read" from the inside.

Early Architectural

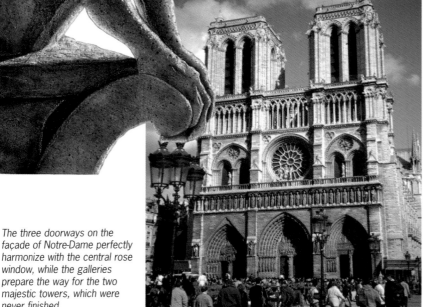

The three doorways on the façade of Notre-Dame perfectly harmonize with the central rose window, while the galleries prepare the way for the two majestic towers, which were never finished.

Notre-Dame

Situated on the Île de la Cité, the Cathedral of Notre-Dame is a resounding example of the magnificence of Gothic architecture. The awesome size of the cathedral is a portrayal of man's desperate need to be close to God, and is realised internally by the use of pointed arches which hold up the vaulted ceilings, and on the outside by extensive arches which contrast with the lateral, flying buttresses. The strong, vertical lines of the cathedral are complemented by the many carvings, sculptures, and stained-glass decorations. Work on the cathedral began in 1163 and continued for 170 years, but in later periods Notre-Dame was subject to many alterations of the choir, sacristy, and spires.

Sainte-Chapelle

Built inside the royal palace of Louis IX (who was also known as Saint Louis) on the Cité as a place to house the precious relics of the Passion, the magnificent Sainte-Chapelle is one of the greatest Gothic architectural masterpieces of the 13th century. The building consists of two superimposed chapels — a lower chapel, destined for public use, and an upper chapel, reserved for the king and the royal family. Known for its luminosity, 15 stained-glass windows, separated by pillars 49 feet (15 m) tall, portray more than 1,000 religious scenes.

Victor Hugo's famous novel about Quasimodo, The Hunchback of Notre-Dame, was published in 1831. The first film was made in 1923 but there have been many remakes. The still (above) shows Anthony Quinn and Gina Lollobrigida in a 1957 version of the doomed love story.

The lower chapel, a large crypt in blue, purple, and gold, has 40 pillars which hold up the weight of the arches and vaulted ceiling.

1678 The Hall of Mirrors at Versailles is begun.

1718 The Elysée Palace, home of French presidents, is built.

1764 Place Louis XV, or Place de la Concorde, is laid out.

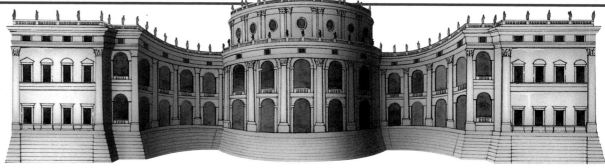

Right: Bernini's design for the Colonnade of the Louvre.

Styles

The Rejected Colonnade

Louis XIV's Colonnade was intended to be the principal entry to the Louvre. Several architects submitted projects for the design of this new structure, including Gianlorenzo Bernini, who in Paris of 1664 was the undisputed master of the Baroque and the mastermind of St. Peter's Square in Rome. He presented a grand project, which was judged too expensive and quickly abandoned. The commission was later given to Claude Perrault who, following Italian traditions in the foundations of the building, built the Colonnade in the Baroque style.

Below: Perrault's Colonnade. It is Baroque in size but Classical in its rigorous, straight lines.

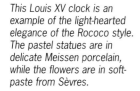

This Louis XV clock is an example of the light-hearted elegance of the Rococo style. The pastel statues are in delicate Meissen porcelain, while the flowers are in soft-paste from Sèvres.

Rococo

In the later years of Louis XIV's reign a new artistic style and taste began to impose itself on society. This was Rococo and it undermined Baroque art. Outstandingly sumptuous, elegant, and sensual, the Rococo style represented the "joie de vivre" (joy of life) of the aristocratic courtier who, after the death of the Sun King, wanted to turn his back on the past and on the oppressive moralism of the last years of the great autocrat. In the early years of Louis XV's reign, especially between 1730 and 1745, the new style was embraced by the upper classes — the aristocracy and the rich bourgeoisie. In these circles Rococo was evident in all aspects of daily life, in painting, literature, fashion, the decorative arts, and above all in interior decoration and architecture.

Madame de Pompadour (1721–64), Louis XV's mistress, was a patron of the Rococo style of painting, fashion, and decorative arts.

Chinese Influence

As Rococo style became more and more exaggerated and excessive, it moved towards the 'exotic' with many unusual decorative ideas. Louis XIV himself commissioned a classic example of Chinese style when, in 1670, he built a Trianon, similar to the Porcelain Tower of Nanking, in the park of Versailles. The taste for Chinese architectural curios was, however, generally limited to theaters, pavilions in public parks, and meeting places. The Universal Exposition of the 19th century used this kind of scenic architecture a lot, but they were removed afterwards.

The Chinese Baths were built in 1787 on the Boulevard des Italiens. There was also a restaurant and café in the baths which were very popular. They were demolished in 1853.

rights of the people against tyrannical governments and religious intolerance. Paris was of central importance to the movement with many of its most influential leaders meeting and writing there. One of the greatest works of the Enlightenment was the *Encyclopedia*, by Jean-Baptiste d'Alembert and Denis Diderot. One of the earliest encyclopedias ever written, its authors tried to present a summary of all human knowledge.

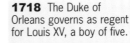

1715 – 1799

1718 The Duke of Orleans governs as regent for Louis XV, a boy of five.

1725 Marriage of Louis XV.

1728 The first street signs (left) appear in Paris.

1763 Peace treaty is signed in Paris with England.

1770 The dauphin, Louis marries Marie-Antoinette.

1774 Louis XVI succeeds to the throne.

The Age of Enlightenment

During the 18th century an intellectual movement known as the Enlightenment spread throughout Europe. Enlightenment thinkers believed in the power of reason and upheld the

Denis Diderot (right), one of the founders of the Encyclopedia, and (above) the title page of the first volume.

Left: A game of tric-trac in a Parisian salon. Intellectuals met to gamble and discuss the ideas of the Enlightenment in salons usually held by wealthy or aristocratic women.

One of 4,500 oil lamps that, from 1764, lit up the streets of Paris.

Revolutionary

Although the court had been in Versailles since 1682, Paris maintained its historical role as the one and only capital of France. The hub of French intellectual life, the city also remained the center stage of political activity. From its beginnings in 1789, Paris was the driving force of the French Revolution and all of the main events of the revolution took place in the city, from the Storming of the Bastille and the conveying of the king from Versailles, to the insurrection that led to the overthrow of the monarchy, the execution of the king, and the main events of the Reign of Terror (1793–94). In the end too, it was the actions of the Parisians that finally halted the Revolution in 1799 and led to Napoleon Bonaparte's rise to power.

The Panthéon

In 1744, to give thanks for his recovery from a serious illness, Louis XV decided to build a basilica dedicated to Sainte Geneviève, patron saint of Paris. The architect Jacques-Germain Soufflot conceived an impressive building in Neoclassical style with a central plan and 22 Corinthian columns that were inspired by the Panthéon in Rome. An iron dome, 272 feet (83 m) high and weighing 10,000 tons, was added and the whole building was reinforced with metal inserted into the brickwork. This enormous structure was transformed into a pantheon (burial place for famous people) during the Revolution, and would become the final resting place of some of France's greatest people. Those buried in the Panthéon include the writers Jean-Jacques Rousseau, Voltaire, Victor Hugo, and Emile Zola. In the 1970s, Jean Moulin, head of the French Resistance during World War II, was also buried there.

The Parisian fire brigade was founded in 1722. At the beginning of the Revolution there were 260 firemen in the city.

Laying the foundation stone at the Panthéon in 1764, where work lasted until 1790.

1782 The first footpaths appear in Rue de l'Odéon.

1786–91 Building of the Wall of the Farmers General around Paris, allows efficient collection of duties on goods entering the city.

1789 (May) Official opening of the Estates-General at Versailles.

(July) Storming of the Bastille.

(August) Declaration of the Rights of Man.

1791 Voltaire is buried in the Panthéon.

1792 Declaration of the French Republic.

1793 Louis XVI and Marie-Antoinette are guillotined.

1794 Robespierre's Reign of Terror begins.

1797 Directory is formed.

1799 Napoleon Bonaparte becomes First Consul.

Times

Flying with Montgolfier

After the Montgolfier brothers' early experiments in Lyons on June 4, 1783, the people of Paris went in masses to watch them launch their balloon in the main squares of the city (far right). On November 21, 1783, Pilâtre de Rozier became hero of the day when he undertook the first human flight. Taking off from the Bois de Boulogne he landed several miles away.

Below: This 18th-century plate decorated with a balloon shows the craze that took hold in France when the first balloon flights took place.

July 14, the day of the Storming of the Bastille, is still the most important national holiday in France.

The Revolution Begins

The people's mounting fury exploded on July 14, 1789 with the attack on the Bastille, state prison and arsenal. Only seven people, all set free, were held in the Bastille at the time, but by the end of the day there were 171 dead (114 of whom had died defending the building). The fortress, built in the 14th century during the reign of Charles V, was the first Parisian monument of the Ancien Régime to be brought to the ground.

The Theater

Going to the theater was a favorite pastime for Parisians and the city already had a strong tradition of theater and opera in the 17th century. The Comédie Française was formed in 1687 and had its first home in what is today the Odéon. In 1784 the first performance of *The Marriage of Figaro* by Beaumarchais took place. By the middle of the 18th century Paris had ten theater halls, a number

The Odéon Theater (left) was built in Neoclassical style by Marie-Joseph Peyre and Charles de Wailly.

which rose to 51 by 1791. Even the people of the Revolutionary period loved theater, especially performances which centered on the fight for liberty from tyrannical governments.

The Neoclassical style of Louis XVI was also evident in the fashion of the period. It was a relatively simple style, composed of a jacket or coat-dress with a short tail and large collar lapels, and a bustle on top of a straight skirt. Some very extravagant hats were worn in this period.

Louis XVI was publically guillotined on January 21, 1793.

Paris — Heart and Mind of the Revolution

Despite the hopes raised by the crowning of a young king in 1774, the monarchy, or Ancien Régime, was in crisis. The state coffers were empty, inflation was rising dramatically, and the majority of Parisians were living in abject poverty. The people's anger exploded on July 14, 1789 with the Storming of the Bastille. Three years later Louis XVI was deposed and France was declared a Republic. The troubles worsened as foreign armies threatened the country's borders, the economic crisis deepened, and the turmoil in Paris increased. Young men were enlisted in the Republican army but 'Liberty, Equality, Fraternity' was not enough to keep alive a city that was lacking in the most basic supplies. Believing the new republic was falling apart, Robespierre imposed his "Reign of Terror" and thousands were sent to the guillotine. Executive power passed to the five-member Directory who planned a series of attacks on Austria. It was during these campaigns that a young, almost unknown general called Napoleon Bonaparte came to the fore.

1800 – 1850

1804 Napoleon crowns himself Emperor of France. The cemeteries of Montparnasse, Père-Lachaise and Montmartre are built.

1806 The first stone of the Arch de Triomphe is laid.

1814 Battle of Paris. The allies enter the city. Napoleon abdicates and the throne is restored to Louis XVIII.

1821 Napoleon dies.

1823 Gas lighting is introduced at Palais-Royal.

1824 Louis XVIII dies and is succeeded by his brother, Charles X.

1830 July Revolution. Abdication of Charles X and Louis-Philippe becomes king.

1831 Sacking of the Palais de la Cité.

1832 Cholera epidemic.

1836 Erection of the Egyptian obelisk from Luxor, Egypt, in the Place de la Concorde.

1839 Daguerre defines his photographic process.

1844 First electric lighting appears in Place de la Concorde.

1845 Restoration work begins on Notre-Dame.

1848 Revolution and the establishment of the Second Republic. Charles Louis Napoleon Bonaparte takes power.

The Departure of the Volunteers in 1792, better known as The Marseillaise, by François Rude, is the most famous statue on the Arch de Triomphe de l'Etoile. Begun in 1806 it was completed in 1836.

Left: The column in Place Vendôme, erected by Napoleon in 1806, was modeled on the Column of Trajan in Rome. Decorated with a spiral of 425 bronze reliefs (which recount the Battle of Austerlitz) forged from enemy canons, it was sculpted by Pierre Bergeret. The statue which originally stood on top of the column showed Napoleon I dressed as Caesar and wearing a laurel crown.

Josephine Bonaparte's bed at the Château de Malmaison is a classic example of Imperial style furniture. It is topped with an Imperial eagle.

Rebuilding the City

Napoleon's reconstruction of Paris involved the demolition of many parts of the medieval city, including the Grand Châtelet in 1802, the Temple Prison in 1808, and the Carmelite Convent in 1813. New structures were erected in their place, such as the Place du Châtelet with its great Palmier Fountain, commissioned by Napoleon in 1807. The new monuments were designed to immortalize the memory of the Emperor and his

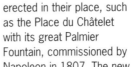

This teapot and sugar bowl from the Parisian Schoelcher factory are decorated with views of Paris.

Precious Objects for the Rich

Paris was a rich city, which both produced and consumed large amounts of everything. In 1807, 31,650 of its 580,000 inhabitants worked in the manufacturing industry, but there were also 2,500 retailers, many of whom dealt in luxury goods. One of the most famous manufacturers was Schoelcher with shops on Boulevard des Italiens. It produced expensive ceramics decorated in gold and polychrome, but was closed down in 1834.

brother, Charles X.

enterprises. The Arch de Triomphe du Carrousel, between the Louvre and the Tuileries gardens, celebrated his military victories, while the Vendôme Column commemorated his victory at the Battle of Austerlitz in 1805. Napoleon also commissioned many projects which were never fulfilled, such as a palace for the king of Rome (his son) which would have stood where the Palais de Chaillot now stands.

Napoleon

The instability of the Directory (the French Revolutionary government, 1795–1799), allowed Napoleon Bonaparte to take power in 1799. Just five years later in 1804 Napoleon had himself crowned Emperor of France in a grand ceremony in the Cathedral of Notre-Dame. His military campaigns redrew the political map of Europe, and Paris, which he wanted to transform into the most beautiful city in the world, was the chosen capital. Ten years of glory ended in 1814 when the forces of Prussia, Austria, and Russia restored the throne to the Bourbons.

This clock (left) in Imperial style was made for the minister Fouché, a government minister both during and after the Revolution. The main clock face is divided into ten minute periods, the time the minister dedicated to each audience.

Napoleon chose the Imperial eagle of Ancient Rome as his symbol.

Napoleon placed a bronze chariot and horses, confiscated by the French from St. Mark's Basilica in Venice, on top of the Arch de Triomphe du Carrousel.

Rue de Rivoli in 1840.

Arcades

The construction of the Palais-Royal galleries in 1786 made shopping arcades the height of fashion and they continued to be popular throughout the Restoration period. Their architecture, revolutionary for the era, included glass roofs held up, in the earliest arcades, by wooden structures and later by metal. Inside there were cafés, shops, and restaurants, very much like a modern shopping mall. The center of Paris quickly filled with arcades, such as the Passage des Panoramas in Boulevard Montmartre, which opened in 1800, and took its name from two large paintings on its walls showing views of Paris. The connecting arcades of Vivienne and Colbert were decorated with symbols of commerce, while the Vétro-Donat arcade, built in 1826, was the first of its kind to use gas lighting.

The Galerie de Orléans in the gardens of the Palais-Royal.

Rue de Rivoli

Commemorating Napoleon's victory in Italy in 1797, Rue de Rivoli was conceived as an east-west axis linking the Louvre with the Champs-Élysées. The wall of the Tuileries gardens was to be replaced with railings. The final plan was made by Auguste-Marie Beudot (1807), who designed houses in Neoclassical style with arches similar to those of Bologna, Padua, and Turin. Building of the street largely took place during the Restoration period with street numbers arriving at today's number of 188 in 1830. The decision to lengthen the street was made in 1848.

and the Restoration

In 1848 the first railway between Paris and Saint-Germain-en-Laye was opened.

The urban plan of medieval Paris with its windy, narrow streets lent itself easily to the erection of barricades during revolts and revolutions. This happened both in July 1830, when Charles X was ousted from the throne, and during the great revolution of 1848, which saw the beginnings of the Second Republic.

A City Suffocating

With almost one million inhabitants squeezed within the customs' walls in 1849, Paris was suffocating. Pressure was placed on city officials to improve infrastructure and roadways of all kinds. As a result 112 new roads were opened, facilitating access to schools, markets, slaughter-houses, and public places. As of 1846 there were 16 omnibus companies working in the city. By 1848 gas lighting covered half the city.

Below: This panoramic view of Paris from the top of the Arch de Triomphe in 1843 shows the two tollhouses of the Étoile barrier, which were demolished in 1860.

A battle on the Arcole Bridge during the Revolution of 1830.

This old Parisian shop sign indicates a bakery or patisserie (pastry shop). Many shop signs in medival Paris were designed so that even those who could not read would know what they would find in the shop.

The Seine has always divided Paris into two distinct worlds. The elegant, wealthy *Rive Droite* (Right Bank) is dedicated to business and has some of the city's most splendid boulevards and monuments. The *Rive Gauche* (Left Bank) is the core of French culture, with the Sorbonne University, as well as many of the city's theaters, cafés, and bookstores. Over the centuries, however, both sides have had their own vibrant street life. Until recently the cries of street pedlars filled the air, and even today the streets outside the elegant boutiques and department stores are filled with artists, buskers, and craftspeople peddling their wares.

This street pedlar sold hot and cold drinks, depending on the season, from the container strapped to his back.

Traditional shop fronts such as this boulangerie (bread shop) can still be seen in many Parisian streets.

THE STREETS OF PARIS

1300 First commercial signs appear above hotels and taverns.

1600s Tobacconist shops begin to be identified by signs printed with the word "tabac."

Street Life in Paris

A milk, cheese, and cream seller.

Les Halles

Until its demolition in 1969, Les Halles had been the central market in Paris since medieval times. Each day tons of perishable food was gathered at Les Halles and sold over the course of 24 hours. In the vegetable, fish, and meat pavilions, food was sold wholesale, while there were also many stalls where peasants displayed their home-grown produce, such as butter, cheese, eggs, and chickens. Alongside the hubbub of people who gathered at Les Halles, the street sellers could always be heard, as the crowds jostled to buy their daily food.

1809 A flower market is created next to the Conciergerie.

The busy street outside of the workroom of Maison Paquin on Rue de la Paix in a painting of c.1902 by Jean Béraud.

A Parisian fishmonger shouts about the freshness of her fish.

The *Midinette*

A common sight on the elegant streets of Paris, where the workshops of the great couturiers (fashion houses) were concentrated, was the *midinette* (right), a young girl whose job it was to deliver clothes and hats to the homes of the rich. Walking quickly through the city streets, a large box tied to her arm with a ribbon, she represented the great fashion houses. Always graceful and smiling, she was expected to dress well without being extravagant, and was often trailed by a young student, soldier, or shop boy hoping to catch her attention.

Flea Markets

Still popular with Parisians and tourists alike, flea markets are found in many parts of the city. Second-hand goods of every sort line the streets, from old coins and huge chandeliers to knick-knacks and broken toys.

A flea market today in the Bastille quarter of Paris.

A man selling a caged parrot on the footpath of a Parisian boulevard at the beginning of the 1900s.

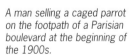

Street Cries

Knife-grinders and roast chestnut sellers, hot and cold drink vendors, hawkers of old clothes and hats, people buying rabbit fur, and dog clippers all crammed the streets of Paris for many years, some up until 50 years ago. They all had their own way of making their presence known and attracting the attention of potential buyers, whether it be a cry at the window of a house, a song, or a nursery-rhyme sung at the top of their voices. The cheeseseller, for example, sang a song which claimed that with her products a housewife was sure to keep hold of her husband!

UNDERGROUND PARIS

1786 The catacombs are established by order of the Lieutenant General of the Police and by the

The ossuary of the Cemetery of St. Laurent, transferred underground in 1859.

Inspector General of Quarries.

1793 Philibert Aspairt, porter of Val-de-Grâce, gets lost and dies in the catacombs, where today there is a tombstone in his memory.

1810 The catacombs become a venue for

fashionable, macabre shows.

1832 A cholera epidemic forces the authorities to build underground sewers.

1854 The first underground

Below: Signs of German occupation in parts of underground Paris during World War II are still visible in some tunnels today.

railway tunnels appear.

1867 The sewers of Paris are opened to the curious.

1870 30,000 wells are dug in the city.

1900 Inauguration of the first metro line.

1903 A fire at the Couronne metro station

claims 84 deaths.

1936 The first underground passage is opened at the Maillot Gate.

1940 The Germans set up a military command center in the tunnel under Rue d'Arras. Members of the Resistance use the one lying under Place Denfert-

Catacombs and Crypts

Between 1785 and 1814, many parts of underground Paris became catacombs when, for reasons of hygiene and overcrowding, more than six million skeletons were moved there from city cemeteries. Some caves,

such as those which lay under the Catholic Institute, were transformed into crypts when the bodies of priests assassinated during the French Revolution were discovered there. Others have been adapted for more secular activities such as that of the Châsse, in Rue Rivoli,

which hosts concerts and exhibitions. Meanwhile the crypt of Saint-André-des-Arts has become a cabaret and the one in Rue Laplace a Russian restaurant.

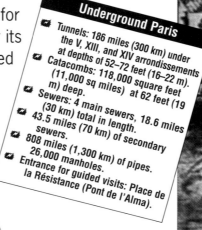

Beneath the City

F aris sinks its roots below the city streets and boulevards to an underground area from which, for centuries, it extracted the materials required for its own construction. Nowadays the upper levels are occupied by a complex system of pipes and tubes carrying the city's gas, water, telephones, heating, electricity, and sewage. Further down, are the rail and metro lines and the road tunnels that link the various parts of Paris and connect the capital to the rest of France.

Underground Paris

- Tunnels: 186 miles (300 km) under the V, XIII, and XIV arrondissements at depths of 52–72 feet (16–22 m).
- Catacombs: 118,000 square feet (11,000 sq miles) at 62 feet (19 m) deep.
- Sewers: 4 main sewers, 18.6 miles (30 km) total in length. 43.5 miles (70 km) of secondary sewers.
- 808 miles (1,300 km) of pipes. 26,000 manholes.
- Entrance for guided visits: Place de la Résistance (Pont de l'Alma).

distilleries in the 12th century, and from 1840, even mushrooms were gathered there. During World War I, the tunnels became underground shelters, and when the Germans occupied Paris during World War II, they installed munition deposits and military bases underground.

Concert in a Crypt

During the Romantic Movement in the 19th century, underground Paris became fashionable, especially after many scenes from Victor Hugo's *Les Misérables*, published in 1862, were set in the city's tunnels and sewers. The mystery and danger of the place attracted those in search of thrills. On the night of April 2, 1897, in the Passion Crypt (also

known as the Shin-Bone Rotunda for the bones that lined its walls and pilasters), 45 musicians held a clandestine concert, which was as sacrilegious as it was scandalous. On the program were Chopin's *Marche Funebre* and Saint-Saëns's *Danse Macabre*. The xylophone is said to have reproduced the noise of grinding bones with great realism!

Above: The underground concert held in Paris in 1897.

The Depths of Paris

Over 186 miles (300 km) of tunnels and quarries lie under Paris, from which gypsum and stone were extracted for years in order to construct the buildings and streets above ground. When the building materials were exhausted, many tunnels and caves became cellars or monastic

Right: A poster from the modern-day musical based on Victor Hugo's Les Miserables.

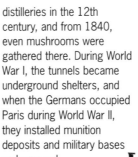

The Sewers

The first underground sewers were built in Paris by the engineer Bruneseau at the beginning of the 19th century. An epidemic of cholera 30 years later, however, showed that the

Rochereau.

1964 The RER begins traveling deeper underground.

1991 The métro system abolishes first class cars.

2001 The NAVIGO urban transport card becomes available in Paris.

The Métro

The Paris metro is one of the largest underground rail systems in the world. It was built following a law passed on March 30, 1896, which declared it to be a project for the Universal Exposition in 1900. Work began under the direction of Fulgence Bienvenüe, chief engineer for the city of Paris. In order to proceed more quickly, the work was divided into lots, although crossing the Seine caused many problems. Sections of the tunnel, which runs under the river, were therefore constructed on land, and once built immersed under water. Bienvenüe finished the line which led to the Exposition center with only a ten day delay, caused by a saboteur who left an iron bar on the tracks.

Underground in the Concorde metro station, where buskers often entertain passengers as they wait for their trains.

sewers were insufficient. When Haussmann began his great works in 1853, the city already had over 62 miles (100 km) of underground pipes, but the new quarters and streets of the city needed an adequate and modern sewage system too. Along with his right-hand man, the engineer Belgrand, Haussmann set about opening a gigantic worksite from which a large part of the present-day sewage network originates.

Left: Workmen enter the underground sewage system from a manhole in a Paris street. Still today, the city's underground pipes and sewers are infested with rats, which vastly outnumber the inhabitants of Paris. City workmen are vaccinated against leptospirosis, a bacterial disease carried by the pests.

Above: A view of life underground from the Place de l'Opera in the early 1900s.

The monuments, streets, historical events, and routines of daily life have inspired artists in Paris since the Middle Ages. Many of their works are valuable historical documents, providing the modern viewer with information on the changing cityscape, architecture, costume, food, and other varied aspects of Paris through the ages. The more subjective paintings, like those of Toulouse-Lautrec and Marc Chagall, offer a glimpse into the moods and idiosyncrasies of a great city and its inhabitants through time.

Paris in Art

1 A Procession of the Catholic League, Place de Grève (c. 1590) *by the French School, 16th century. This procession occurred during one of the most tragic periods of Parisian history: the Wars of Religion.*

2 Paris Through the Window, 1913, *painted by Marc Chagall.*

3 Dance at the Moulin Rouge, *painted by Henri Toulouse-Lautrec at the end of the 19th century.*

4 Tour Eiffel 1910, 1911. *Robert Delaunay's Eiffel Tower painted in 1911.*

5 *The officer and the midinette, familiar characters on the Parisian boulevard during the Second Empire, in* the painting The Boulevard of the Capucines and the Vaudeville Theatre, 1889 *by Jean Béraud.*

6 *A detail of the center of Paris in the* Très Riches Heures *painted by the Limbourg Brothers in the 15th century.*

7 *The Pont Neuf "wrapped" by the artist Christo in 1985.*

8 Liberty Leading the People *by Eugène Delacroix.*

4

8

The Opening Ceremony

The Eiffel Tower was opened to the public on May 15, 1889 and was immediately an enormous success, despite the initial reservations of Parisian intellectuals. Although the lifts were not in working order that day (they began working six days later), 28,922 visitors climbed the tower on foot to reach the first and second platforms. A craze for souvenirs of the tower exploded almost straight away, which included miniature towers, bottles, candles, trinkets and

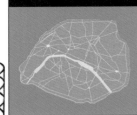

greetings cards, paper-weights, and lamps, all of which were sold in the new Printemps department store.

The most eager visitors to the Eiffel Tower, who packed the entrance hall from dawn, did not hesitate to climb the dangerous, winding staircase to the second platform.

1850 – 1900

1851 The station of Saint-Lazare is built.

1855 The church of Saint-Eugène is the first religious building to be built of cast iron.

1863 The Gare du Nord is built, one of the first examples of the joint use of iron and glass.

1874 Baltard and Callet finish building Les Halles.

1875 The reading room of the National Library is opened. Its iron structure reduces the danger of fire.

1887 Work begins on the Eiffel Tower.

1889 The Eiffel Tower is opened, focal point of the 1889 Universal Exposition.

1896 The difficult work on Pont Mirabeau is completed.

1900 The Alexander III bridge and the Grand Palais are opened. The tower of the Electricity Palace is encircled at its base by a sumptuous glass structure.

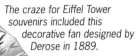

The craze for Eiffel Tower souvenirs included this decorative fan designed by Derose in 1889.

The Era of Glass and Metal

The spread of the Industrial Revolution and mass culture in the second half of the 19th century gave rise to vast industrial fairs, or Universal Expositions, which inspired architects to explore the use of materials and techniques that were in step with the times. The result was light, transparent structures in glass and iron, that could be erected, and demolished, quickly. The use of iron meant that elements could be prefabricated in workshops and then assembled at the designated location. The introduction of steel, welding, perforated bricks, and reinforced concrete allowed these buildings to reach great heights, and they became symbols of modern times.

Mr Eiffel's Tower

In preparation for the Universal Exposition of 1889, on May 1, 1886 the Ministry of Commerce and Industry called tenders for projects to build "an iron tower with a square base, 410 feet (125 m) wide, and 985 feet (300 m) tall." Of the 107 projects tendered, that of the engineer Gustave Eiffel was chosen. His company already enjoyed a solid reputation in the field of metallic construction, having

made railroad viaducts and arched bridges in many parts of the world, not to mention the framework of the famous Statue of Liberty which was unveiled in 1886 in New York. The building site opened in Champ-de-Mars on January 8, 1887 and after 700 days the Eiffel Tower (right) was opened to its first visitors.

Notre-Dame-du-Travail

There were other churches in Paris made of iron, but Jules Astruc's Notre-Dame-du-Travail (1899–1901) was the first to use industrial iron girders, which are riveted and welded together. This, combined with the high windows above its spacious interior, made it seem spare and functional, more like the factories in which the parishioners of this working-class suburb spent their days.

Left: Inside Notre-Dame-du-Travail the iron girders were exposed above the aisles.

The Eiffel Tower in Numbers

- ✔ Height: 1054 feet (320 m), including the antenna.
- ✔ 1652 steps to reach the third floor.
- ✔ Constructed of 18,000 metal pieces held together by 2.5 million rivets.
- ✔ Maximum of 4.7 inches (12 cm) oscillation.
- ✔ Weight 10,100 tons.
- ✔ To paint the tower (every four years) 40 tons of paint are used.
- ✔ Three platforms at 187, 377, and 899 feet (57, 115, 274m).
- ✔ In the 177 days of the Exposition 1,953,122 visitors visited the tower.
- ✔ In 100 years there have been 120 million visitors.

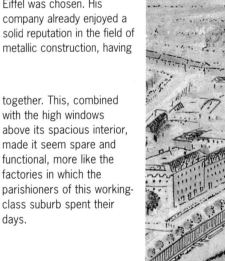

Saint-Lazare Station by Impressionist artist Claude Monet. The immense structure of iron and glass was defined by the writer Théophile Gautier as "a cathedral of the new humanity."

Building a Bridge under Water

The Mirabeau bridge is built of two symmetrical metal frames which form a 328 feet (100m) arch. Its construction (1893–96) was both difficult and dangerous because for the first time in Paris the excavators worked in air compressed water-tanks that rested on the riverbed.

An arch of the Mirabeau bridge.

Alexander III Bridge and the Grand Palais

At the Universal Exposition of 1900, the most elegant bridge in Paris was put on show — the Alexander III bridge was built to celebrate the Franco-Russian alliance and was dedicated to its namesake, Tsar Alexander III. In Art Nouveau style, it was richly decorated with gold statues (below right) and lamp-posts like those in St. Petersburg. It stretched 358 feet (109 m) across the Seine River between the Left Bank and the Grand Palais. Also built for the Universal Exposition, the Grand Palais, with its Neoclassical stone façade, is decorated in wrought iron and covered with a large glass dome supported by an iron frame. Illuminated from the inside at night, it creates a spectacular effect

The Grand Palais stands on the Right Bank and can be seen from the Alexander III bridge.

Les Halles

Writer Emile Zola called Les Halles, the great Parisian food market, "the belly of Paris," because all the produce consumed in the city was sold there. In 1851 Napoleon III commissioned the architect Baltard to build ten iron pavilions, each covered by giant glass skylights with cast-iron columns, near the church of Saint-Eustache. The effect was to create a single vast interior space where fish, meat, cheese, butter, and vegetables were sold.

In 1969 the market was moved to Rungis 9 miles (15 km) south of the city. All the pavilions were demolished, apart from two, one of which was reassembled in Yokohama, Japan.

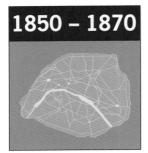

1850 – 1870

1851 Coup d'état by Louis Napoleon Bonaparte.

1852–70 The most famous department stores of the capital open.

1853 Haussmann is named prefect of the Seine département and begins his transformation of Paris.

1855 Universal Exposition.

1856 Great festivities in the public squares to celebrate the birth of the Emperor's son.

1857 The tailor Worth opens a workshop in Rue de la Paix. Paris begins to be known as a fashion capital.

1859 Demolition of the tollhouse at the Clichy barrier.

1860 The inner suburbs are annexed to the capital, which passes from 12 to 20 arrondissements.

1861 Work begins on the sewers at La Villette and Les Halles. Paris is in uproar for

the arrival of the Ambassador of the King of Siam.

1862 Work begins on the Opéra. In Boulevard Strasbourg the Grand Café opens its doors.

1867 New Universal Exposition.

1870 Napoleon is defeated at Sedan and the Third Republic is proclaimed.

The Opéra — Symbol of the Second Empire

Among the 170 projects for the Théâtre de l'Opéra, which Napoleon III wanted to build as a symbol of the opulence of his empire, that of a young unknown, Charles Garnier, was chosen. The building's unique appearance is a result of the combination of different materials (among which marble, stone, copper, and bronze), and architectural styles (from Classical to Baroque), in a profusion of columns, friezes, and sculpture. Inside, a grand, white marble staircase with red and green marbled balustrades leads into the Grand Foyer with its mosaic decorated dome, and the auditorium, a triumph of red velvet, cherubs, and gilt. The building of the Opéra began in 1862, but was only finished in 1875, five years after the fall of the Second Empire. Napoleon III never saw his opera house finished.

Below the Opéra lies a small lake which the writer Gaston Leroux suggested was the hiding place of his famous character — the Phantom of the Opera.

The Second Empire

Portrait of Napoleon III.

Napoleon III's court took up residence in the Tuileries Palace, which overlooked the Louvre.

Paris lived through a second revolution in 1848, when King Louis-Philippe was overthrown and a new republic was established. This led to the rise of Louis Napoleon Bonaparte, who proclaimed himself Napoleon III, Emperor of France. During this Second Empire period, the medieval, semi-rural city of Paris was transformed into the modern, commercial capital that we know today, and also into one of the most beautiful cities in Europe.

The sewage system was completely renovated by the engineer, Eugène Belgrand, and was extended from 99 to 385 miles (160 to 620 km).

Growth of the Suburbs

Between 1859 and 1860, 11 villages, including Montmartre, were annexed to Paris. This brought the number of arrondissements to 20 and the city's population to 1.8 million. At the same time, Parisians began moving out to the suburbs and built villas and cottages. Largely available only to the more affluent classes, the most favored suburbs were in the west near to the Bois de Boulogne. With developments in transport, suburbs such as Passy and Auteuil saw a steady growth in population, as Parisians sought freedom from the constraints of city life.

Another Bonaparte in Power

Napoleon I's nephew, Louis Napoleon Bonaparte (1808–73) was elected president of France in 1848. By the end of 1852, however, he had declared himself Emperor Napoleon III, a success which was largely due to his name. Together with his wife, the Empress Eugenie, Napoleon III established a fashionable, luxurious court. Noted for her extravagance, the empress employed the best *haute couture* designers and entertained the cream of political and artistic society at magnificent balls and dinners.

One of the bronze lampposts standing outside the Opéra.

The Gare de l'Est was built between 1847 and 1850.

An omnibus of the Bastille-Madeleine line.

Ladies choosing gloves at Bon Marché (right) and the magnificent central hall of Le Printemps (below).

Transportation

Between 1850 and 1870 a railroad network was built that allowed the efficient transportation of people and goods to every part of France. The network, managed by six private companies all equipped with modern steam trains, was centered on Paris. Each company served a different part of France and they all had their own station in Paris. Haussmann also introduced two suburban railways; the larger one was used for transporting goods while the smaller one carried passengers to and from suburbs such as Auteuil, which had been englobed by the capital. Within the city, there were 31 horse-drawn omnibus routes or steam trams, although the city was already beginning to think of an underground railway like the one opened in London in 1863. Goods and merchandise, however, continued to be transported, at least until 1867, on barges that plied the Seine.

A Shoppers' Paradise

The Second Empire also saw the rise of the *grands magasins* (department stores) in Paris. These stores sold everything — from elegant clothing to dusters, linen tablecloths to boxes of matches, and suites of bedroom furniture to lowly stools — at fixed prices. With several floors, entrance was free, and customers could look at the goods on display without necessarily buying anything. Shop assistants were expected to be friendly and smiling, despite their grueling 15-hour work days. The ladies of Paris were highly enthusiastic about these new stores and often met in Au Bon Marché, opened in 1852, Le Printemps, popular since its opening in 1865, and the Samaritaine, which opened its doors in 1870.

VUE du HALL CENTRAL des NOUVEAUX MAGASINS DU PRINTEMPS
Ce Hall octogonal, large de 25 mètres, est couronné à 50 mètres de hauteur, par un dôme d'une prodigieuse hardiesse, support d'une éblouissante verrière.

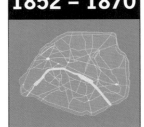

1852 (March) A Parliamentary decree authorizes the expropriation of land and property to the discretion of the government.

1852–69 19,718 houses are demolished and 43,777 new houses are built.

1854 An Imperial decree imposes precise rules on architects regarding the height and façade of buildings.

1855 The Alma Bridge and the extension of Rue de Rivoli is completed.

1858 Boulevard Sébastopol is opened.

1860 Building of the church of Saint-Augustin on Boulevard Malesherbes begins.

1861 Boulevard Malesherbes is opened. Rebuilding of the Gare du Nord.

Before Haussmann

From the Restoration up until the era of Haussmann's transformation, the state of the streets of Paris was

A degraded street of the old center of Paris. Passage d'Harcourt disappeared under the axes of the Second Empire.

endlessly discussed in the press and in novels (the writer Balzac was particularly critical). Many complained about the narrow, dirty streets in the old city center, and of the lack of fresh water. Even in middle class areas, water was still distributed by water-

carriers who shouted loudly to announce their arrival.

The Prefect

Georges-Eugène, Baron Haussmann (1809–91) was prefect of the Seine from 1853 until 1870. Before that he was subprefect of Nérac, where he built an efficient network of roads, bridges, and canals, and founded the first public schools. Many criticized Haussmann for destroying too much of the old city, but this did not stop him. He demolished houses without remorse, including his own birthplace in the Beaujon quarter. Today one of his boulevards, which begins in Étoile, bears his name — Boulevard Haussmann.

Water-carriers were expected to lug buckets of water up to the top floors of Paris apartment blocks.

Haussmann's

E ntrusted by the emperor Napoleon III to modernize Paris, in the 1850s Haussmann started what was probably the largest urban renewal project the world has ever seen. The project was focused especially on the Left Bank which had maintained its medieval character compared to the Right Bank, which was expanding rapidly to the west. Large open spaces were created, with new parks and wide, straight, tree-lined boulevards. In this grand transformation, many of the old, medieval buildings of the city were destroyed, especially on the Île de la Cité, where almost all the densely-packed buildings were demolished.

The great crossroads in a map of 1864. It was formed by the north-south Sébastopole-St-Michel and the east-west axis which extended from Rue de Rivoli to the Place de la Bastille.

Haussmann's Work

An old Parisian dream of developing a great road network was put into effect by Haussmann. Opening up new avenues, demolishing old areas like the insalubrious Hôtel de Ville and Grand Châtelet, he

developed large, new squares and well-aligned houses and buildings. He also razed the medieval houses of the Île de la Cité in order to enlarge the churchyard of Notre-Dame. In modernizing the city's infrastructure, he succeeded in piping fresh water, which in 1852 had only reached the lower floors of 6,000 houses, into 34,000 houses, even up to the top floors.

Demolition work in Boulevard du Temple around 1857.

1862 Boulevard Saint-Michel is born.

1864 Urban renewal in the Cité is finished. Work begins in the Avenue de l'Opéra, carried out in stages until 1878.

1870 Haussmann resigns.

At rich houses concierges (doorpeople) were expected to mop the street outside their buildings, a chore forced upon them by police decree.

A busy scene near the Café Tortoni on Boulevard des Italiens in 1856.

Open Spaces

The Arch and the Star

Napoleon III had asked Haussmann to converge four avenues on the Arch de Triomphe (right), to cross the Champs-Elysées and its extension, the Avenue de la Grande-Armée. The Baron, however, had grander ideas. The design for the Place de l'Étoile, with its 12 streets radiating out from the Arch de Triomphe, was without doubt his greatest work. The 1.25 miles (2 km) of the Champs-Elysées, bordered by parks with fountains and pavilions, became the epitome of luxury and elegance during the Belle Époque.

Below: A boulevard buffet where gentlemen could buy cigars and ladies little bottles of rose water to help them cool down during their strolls.

Long and Straight

Running right across the city, Haussmann's streets were chiefly built to solve the traffic problem, but they also served to connect the city to the railway stations which, in turn, linked Paris to the provinces. Where the landscape permitted, the streets were cut in long, straight avenues, such as the Avenue de l'Opéra, often linking squares or open spaces across the city (Concorde–Étoile, Place de la Bastille–Panthéon).

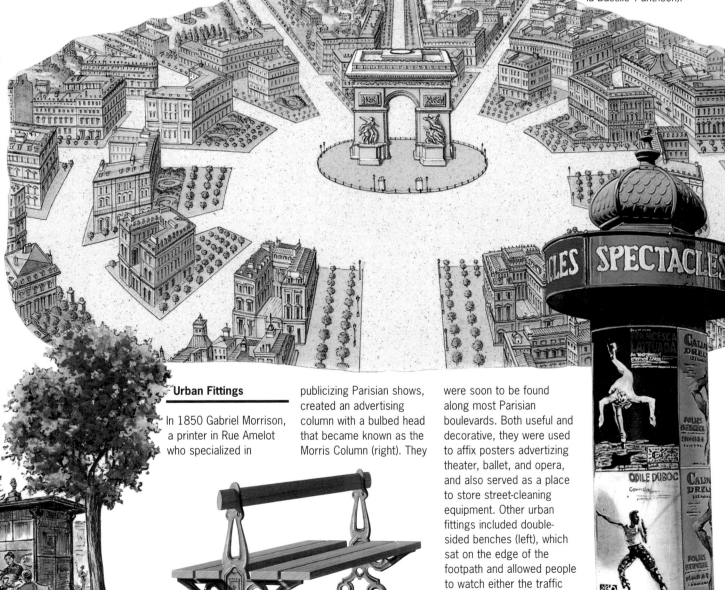

Urban Fittings

In 1850 Gabriel Morrison, a printer in Rue Amelot who specialized in publicizing Parisian shows, created an advertising column with a bulbed head that became known as the Morris Column (right). They were soon to be found along most Parisian boulevards. Both useful and decorative, they were used to affix posters advertizing theater, ballet, and opera, and also served as a place to store street-cleaning equipment. Other urban fittings included double-sided benches (left), which sat on the edge of the footpath and allowed people to watch either the traffic on the road or the pedestrians who passed by on the other side.

The Prussian Siege of Paris lasted for five months. Food was scarce and long lines formed outside bakeries and food shops all over the city.

1870–71 Siege of Paris by Prussian troops.

1871 Paris Commune.

1872 Reconstruction of the Hôtel de Ville.

1875 The Opéra opens.

1876 Work on the Basilica of Sacré-Cœur begins.

1878 Universal Exposition.

1884 Paris is provided with garbage bins, known as "poubelles" from the name of the prefect who installed them.

1888 The Pasteur Institute is established.

1889 Universal Exposition to celebrate the 100th anniversary of the French Revolution.

1890 The Moulin Rouge opens its doors.

1895 At the Grand Café on Boulevard des Capucines, the Lumière brothers present their first

cinematografic show.

1898 The Dreyfus Affair explodes — in which a Jewish officer is wrongly accused of selling military secrets to the Prussians.

1899 Louis Renault produces the first car with a three-speed gearbox.

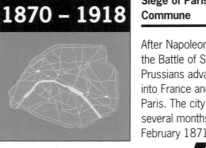

1870 – 1918

Siege of Paris and the Commune

After Napoleon's defeat at the Battle of Sedan the Prussians advanced rapidly into France and laid siege to Paris. The city resisted for several months, but in February 1871 the French government signed an armistice with the Prussians. This was too much for the working people of Paris; they revolted and on March 10, 1871 the socialist Commune of Paris was set up and declared Paris a free city. The Commune was brutally repressed at the end of May by the national government.

The French national sporting passion for cycling developed at the turn of the 20th century. The demanding Paris-Brest-Paris race and the first Tour de France in 1903 launched the career of Maurice Garin, originally a chimney-sweep.

The Belle Époque

The early period of the Third Republic was a difficult time for Paris, with the Prussian siege of the city followed by the Commune of Paris and its ferocious repression. The city, however, quickly healed its wounds, and once again took on the role of world cultural center, a position it had held since the 17th century and which Napoleon III had strengthened. This relatively carefree and confident time for Paris is known simply as the Belle Époque ("beautiful time").

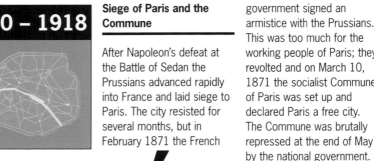

Theater

Alongside the classical pieces performed at the Comédie Française, and the huge success of the actress Sarah Bernhardt at the Odéon, many smaller theaters were also operating. They produced comedies for the middle class, rather like today's TV soap operas in style and content. During Haussmann's work, the Boulevard du Temple with its many theaters, was destroyed to make room for the Place de la République.

A theater poster in Art Nouveau style for a Sarah Bernhardt show.

The entrance to the Mètro at Les Abbesses, designed by Hector Guimard.

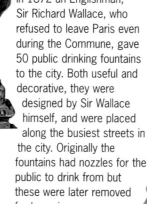

The Wallace fountains are 8.2 feet (2.5 m) tall. Today 66 fountains can still be found in various locations around the city.

Sir Richard's Fountains

In 1872 an Englishman, Sir Richard Wallace, who refused to leave Paris even during the Commune, gave 50 public drinking fountains to the city. Both useful and decorative, they were designed by Sir Wallace himself, and were placed along the busiest streets in the city. Originally the fountains had nozzles for the public to drink from but these were later removed for hygenic reasons.

The Métro

The first underground railroad line (or "Métro" as the Parisians call it) was opened in 1900 for the Universal Exposition. Every ten minutes, three carriages traveling at 22.3 mph (36 km/h) linked eight stations:

Port de Vincennes, Place de la Nation, Gare de Lyon, Place de la Bastille, Hôtel de Ville, Palais-Royal, Champs-Elysées, and Porte Maillot. The stations and their entranceways were designed in the new Art Nouveau style.

All Under the Same Roof

At the beginning of the 19th century, the dividing line between middle and working class Parisians was unclear. In the tall Paris apartment buildings, where the floors were linked by the backstairs, many different social classes were gathered under the same roof. Humble laborers and dressmakers might live on the mezzanine floor, while the spacious first and second floors were occupied by the wealthy. The third floor was home to modest office clerks and servants, while penniless artists and working class families lived in the attic.

Art Nouveau

With its supple, curved lines, Art Nouveau represented objects and human bodies in a strongly stylized way. Artists used "unusual" materials, such as reinforced concrete, glass, and cast iron. They also wanted the new style to be a part of daily life, so Art Nouveau became typical of all aspects of the Belle Époque, from urban design, to fashion, and furniture.

Right: A classic example of Art Nouveau — the doorway of 29 Avenue Rapp, near the Eiffel Tower.

1900 The Universal Exposition marks the start of a new century. The Sorbonne is rebuilt.

1904 A 'cordial agreement' is drawn up between France and Great Britain.

1907 Russia unites with France and Great Britain to form the Triple Alliance.

1909 Louis Blériot carries out the first flight across the Channel in 37 minutes. Diaghilev's Russian Ballet arrives in Paris.

1910 The Seine floods. Work on Sacré-Cœur is completed.

1913 The Champs-Élysées Theater opens.

1914 France enters World War I.

1914 (September) German troops arrive at Marne, 12 miles (20 km) from Paris. The reservists are transported to the Front in taxis.

1918 The Armistice ends World War I.

Parisian Newspapers

A law of July 29, 1881 conceded extensive freedom to publishers in France. There were more than 15 daily newspapers, including *Le Temps*, *Le Figaro*, and *L'Humanité*, representing all political parties, from the socialists on the left to the nationalistic right. Popular press such as *La Presse* and *Le Siècle* published classified advertisements, and to stay popular with their readers, they dedicated large amounts of space to *feuilleton*, or novels published in weekly or fortnightly episodes.

World Fair of 1900

☑ **Opening:** April 14 in the presence of the President of the Republic, Émile Loubet.

☑ **Development:** 272 acres (110 h) on both banks of the Seine from Champ-de-Mars to the Invalides Bridge and along the Champs-Élysées.

☑ **Monuments built:** Alexander III Bridge, the Petit and Grand Palais.

☑ **Arrival Points:** the new stations of d'Orsay and Invalides.

☑ **Visitors:** 50.8 million: the most important was the Tsar Nicolas II.

☑ **Exhibitors:** 83,000.

EXPOSITION UNIVERSELLE DE PARIS 1900

Postcard of the World Fair in Paris in 1900.

The Citroën 5CV began to be seen in 1900. Very soon car racing became as popular as cycling races.

World Fairs

Paris hosted World Fairs in 1855, 1867, 1889, and again in 1900. International exhibitions of this type provide an opportunity for countries to demonstrate their technological progress and the city that hosts them becomes, for a few months at least, a showcase for the world. The World Fair (*L'Exposition de Paris*) of 1889, held to celebrate the centenary of the French Revolution, was an especially exciting occasion. The Eiffel Tower was built, and the Champ-de-Mars and the hill of Chaillot areas where it was held were set out in Art Nouveau style. Ten years later, the World Fair of 1900, which celebrated the dawn of the 20th century, was even more spectacular than its predecessor. It was entirely lit with recently invented electric lighting.

The First Movie

On December 28, 1895, a handful of curious spectators entered a darkened room in the Grand Café on the Boulevard des Capucines and saw an enormous, puffing train appear on a white screen. It seemed so true-to-life that they were both shocked and excited. This was the dawn of the movies, invented by two brothers, Louis and Auguste, whose surname — Lumière (meaning "light") seemed particularly appropriate. The cinema notice (above) advertises the first comedy film ever: *The Waterer Watering!*

The Belle Époque was not just a time of frivolity and wealth. The art world was in turmoil, with Symbolist painters such as Redon and Moreau and sculptors like Rodin revolutionizing the visual arts. Politics were no less lively, with anarchists and revolutionaries drumming up violence in the streets and threatening the already shaky Republic. With hindsight, it was a period that contained the seeds of many of the tragic events of the 20th century.

An advertisement for the Moulin Rouge which, together with the Folies-Bergère and the Ba-Ta-Clan, were the temples of can-can, the dance which took Paris by storm during the Belle Époque.

Women's Fashion

Some of the largest fashion houses opened during the Belle Époque. In 1906, the young tailor Paul Poiret started a virtual revolution — he realised just how uncomfortable women's clothes really were with their tight corsets, boning, large skirts, and underskirts. He set about inventing a "free" dress which later became the symbol of female emancipation (left). In just a few years, women's fashion underwent a rapid transformation. In 1911 Coco Chanel, one of the most famous Parisian dressmakers, invented the cloche hat and in 1914 dramatically shortened women's skirts.

Above: One of the most important Impressionist paintings, The Moulin de la Galette, by Auguste Renoir (1883).

Of Roman-Byzantine inspiration, the Basilica of the Sacré-Coeur was designed by Paul Abadie. Its dome is the highest point in Paris after the Eiffel Tower.

The Montmartre café-concert

At the Café Le Mirliton, Aristide Bruant, the ferociously satirical, anarchic singer, entertained the public in a hunting jacket, red shoes, and a revolutionary hat. At the very heart of Montmartre café-concert society, he was the subject of many Toulouse-Lautrec posters of the period.

A famous poster by Toulouse-Lautrec showing Aristide Bruant.

No real gentleman could appear in public without a top-hat during the Belle Époque. It was a fashion that was imposed with much publicity, such as this advertisement for a hatmaker in Paris.

A Vow to Save France

At the beginning of the Franco-Prussian war in 1870, two businessmen, Alexandre Legentil and Rohault de Fleury, took a vow to make amends for France's wrongdoings and save Paris from a Prussian siege. They collected money to build a basilica dedicated to the Sacred Heart of Jesus on the hill of Montmartre. The work began in 1875 and only finished in 1914, at the beginning of World War I. The consecration of the Basilica of the Sacré-Coeur (left) was therefore delayed until 1919.

The Decorative Arts

Floral designs were all the rage in home furnishings, accessories and trimmings for clothing, poster illustrations, and jewelry throughout this period.

Impressionism

With the advent of photography, paintings could no longer just reproduce reality, and artists sought a new way of representing the world. Some began to experiment with light and color and this led to the Impressionist movement. The movement gained recognition when an exhibition of paintings opened in the studio of the photographer Nadar on April 15, 1874. The artists exhibiting included Renoir, Manet, Monet, Cézanne, Pissarro, Sisley, and Van Gogh. The movement took its name from a painting by Monet called *Impression, Soleil Levant.*

An elaborate candlestick from 1900.

Natural designs, based on flowers, leaves, insects, tendrils, and many other features of the natural world, were all popular.

MEETING PLACES

1617 Luxembourg Gardens are opened.

1633 Louis XIII creates the Jardin des Plantes.

1666 André Le Notre transforms the Tuileries gardens of Catherine de Medicis.

1775 The Count of Artois, the future King Charles X, builds the Bagatelle at Bois de Boulogne.

1778 The gardens of the Latin quarter open to the public.

1787 The Duke of Chartres, the future King Louis-Philippe, constructs Monceau, the first Anglo-Chinese garden.

1857 Napoleon III creates the Bois di Vincennes.

1867 Buttes-Chaumont park opens in the northeast of Paris, an example of a Haussmanian park. The gardens of the Observatory are created, recently renamed "Robert-Cavalier-de-La Salle" and "Marco Polo".

1878 Montsouris park replaces Buttes-Chaumont park in the south of the city.

1882 After the removal of the remains of the Tuileries palace, the gardens of the Carrousel are created.

1954 Raymond Berthillon presents his customers with 72 flavors of ice-cream on the Île Saint-Louis.

1969 Vincennes park opens, center of horticultural shows.

1987 Architect Bernard Tschumi plans Villette park.

1988 Belleville park opens.

2000 Hot air balloon rides over Parc André-Citroën to celebrate the new Millennium.

Parisians meet in cafès, bistrots, restaurants, gardens, salons, and many other places too. Meeting friends, seeing people, and being seen, have always been favorite pastimes in Paris, even though social mores and customs have changed over the centuries. Places that were the height of fashion 50 years ago have disappeared, along with their trademark accordion music and sentimental songs. They have been replaced by more modern meeting places, such as bars, clubs, and restaurants. However, throughout the city, in public gardens, along the banks of the Seine, and in the cafés and bistrots that line the streets and boulevards, Parisians of all classes continue to meet today.

Cafés and Bistrots

Ever since the first café, Le Procope, opened in 1686, the café has been a central part of daily life in Paris. Parisians go to cafés to meet their friends, have a drink, read newspapers, write letters (and novels), talk business, or simply to watch the world go by. Some cafés attract people with the same interests, such as chess, billiards, or cards, while others are known for their famous clients: *Les Deux Magots* and the *Flore* were favorites with Sartre and Simone de Beauvoir; *La Coupole* was Hemingway's hideaway; whereas Salvador Dali and Jean Cocteau preferred *Le Sélect*. There are also bistrots throughout the city where customers can sip a glass of pastis or wine and have a baguette (sandwich). The bistrot shown opposite was depicted by Léonard Foujita in 1958.

The Seine River

The Seine, which meanders for 7.5 miles (12 km) through the city center, is regarded as the most beautiful street in Paris. André Gide wrote that it was "the soul of the city," the famous music-hall artist Mistinguett said that it was "a beautiful blonde with smiling eyes," while Yves Montand called it a "source of inebriation." Magnificent palaces, elegant houses, monuments, museums, and gardens reflect onto its waters, as tourists pass by on *bateaux mouches*.

A Place

Maria de Medicis' Florentine Garden

In the 16th century, Maria de Medicis, widow of King Henri IV, had an Italian palace built in what was then the countryside. Along with the palace, she had gardens designed that were similar to the Boboli gardens in Florence, where she had spent much of her happy childhood. In the meantime the Florentine influence has vanished due to constant remodellings over the years. The Luxembourg Gardens, as they are known today, were opened to the public in 1642. The gardens have a classical structure, with long, shady

On July 21 2002, the riverbank of the Seine, from the Eiffel Tower to the Louvre, was transformed into a beach. For a month, sand, potted palm trees, chairs, sun loungers, and entertainers lined the riverbanks.

The Bois de Boulogne

On the eastern edge of Paris stands the Bois de Boulogne, with its 2,100 acres (850 h) of woodland, 142,000 trees, 22 miles (35 km) of paved footpaths, and 18 miles (29 km) of horse-riding paths. The preferred destination for Parisian picnics and outings, the park was created during the Second Empire. It immediately became the place for the wealthy to take the air in their carriages, under the envious stares of the less privileged Parisians, who were there to enjoy the open-air dance halls, taverns, and eating-houses provided for them. One of the best-loved places was the Bagatelle, a small castle built for the queen, Marie-Antoinette, where a splendid rose garden was planted in 1905. The Bois also has the Pré-Catelan, a 3,000-seat

Children have sailed their toy boats in the central pond of the Luxembourg gardens for centuries.

theater and the Shakespeare Gardens, where all the plants mentioned in the playwright's work are grown. The cycling scene (below) was painted by Jean Béraud in the early 20th century.

to Meet

elm walkways, smooth lawns, fountains, flower beds, and statues of the queens of France (originally intended to help explain the history of France to children who played in the gardens).

The gardens have greenhouses with exotic flowers, bowling greens, tennis courts, cafés, puppet theaters, and pony rides. In front of the building's main pavilion, there is a large, octagonal swimming pool, with chairs and sun loungers arranged around it.

Above: An oriental temple in the Bois de Boulogne.

Louis XIV's court officials take a walk in the Tuileries gardens.

The Oldest Public Garden in Paris

The first Tuileries gardens were laid out around Catherine de Medicis' palace in the 16th century. During the reign of Louis XIV, the architect and landscaper André Le Notre, head of the royal gardens, transformed the Tuileries gardens into Neoclassical style, with large central walkways, terraces, and arabesque flower beds at regular intervals. It gave the impression of an open air salon in which the public could watch, from a distance, king and courtiers as they took their daily walk. The public were allowed admission on condition that they behaved decorously and wore their Sunday best. When Louis XIV moved to Versailles, the gardens became an oasis in the growing city, complete with cafés, refreshment booths, and stone benches to rest on during afternoon strolls.

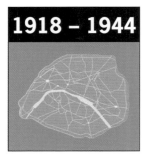

1918 – 1944

1920 The first low income houses are built (HBM: habitation à bon marché).

1921 Demolition of the old fortifications.

1922 Radio programs are distributed by a transmitter on top of the Eiffel Tower. There are 200 cinema halls in Paris.

1925 The population of Paris is three million.

1926 Art Déco appears in the iron and glass structure of the department store, La Samaritaine.

1928 Coco Chanel drastically shortens women's skirts. Pierre Chareau builds the first house with glass walls and a steel framework.

1930 Network of gas pipes is laid.

1931 Colonial exhibition at the Bois de Vincennes.

1936 Devaluation of the currency.

1937 World Fair. The two great totalitarian states, the Soviet Union and Nazi Germany, also take part. Creation of the Museum of Man at the Palais de Chaillot.

1938 International display of Surrealist art.

1940–44 German occupation.

1944 (August) Liberation.

Right: Russian ballet dancers in a poster of the period.

The architecture of the 1930s was ornamental in the extreme, as the tower of the Rex cinema shows (below). Situated on Boulevard Poissonnière, it was built in 1930.

The Russian Ballet

Diaghilev's Russian Ballet Company performed almost continually between 1909 and 1929. It was the first, true expression of modern ballet, and created enormous enthusiasm. The theatrical gazette could speak of nothing else, while Parisians besieged the Châtelet Theater from dawn to get a ticket for the show.

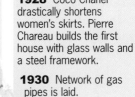

1920s women's fashion included long-waisted dresses, which floated around the hips, like on this Patou model.

City of Light

Paris is also known as *La ville lumière,* or the "City of Light," perhaps because of the brilliance of the World Fair in 1900. Whatever its origins, Paris certainly lived up to its name in the 1920s and 1930s, when it was truly the world capital of art, music, literature, fashion, and love of life. It was home to everyone from exiled kings and influential politicians, to avantguard artists and budding novelists. The lights were dimmed, however, in 1940 when the Nazis occupied the city.

Cabaret Stars

In 1924 a young American dancer named Josephine Baker arrived in Paris with *La Revue Nègre,* a group of jazz musicians and dancers from Harlem, New York. They were wildly successful and Josephine stayed on to appear at the Folies Bergère in 1926–27 where, with her Banana Dance and many others, she took Paris and Europe by storm. Equally popular were the French comedienne, Mistinguett (1875–1956), who achieved her greatest fame at the Moulin Rouge and Casino de Paris, and Maurice Chevalier, the comedian and singer, who became a star of the French music halls.

The Paris Olympics

Between May and July 1924, in extremely high temperatures, Paris hosted the Olympic Games for the second time, after those of 1900. Forty-four nations and 3,093 athletes took part, of whom 136 were women. Germany, however, was noticeably absent, as it continued to settle its war debts.

Despite France winning a total of 36 medals, the real heroes of the Paris Olympics of that year were the Finnish long-distance runner, Paavo Nurmi and the American swimmer, Johnny Weissmuller, who later shot to fame in the role of Tarzan, King of the Jungle.

Left: A poster for the 1924 Olympic Games in Paris.

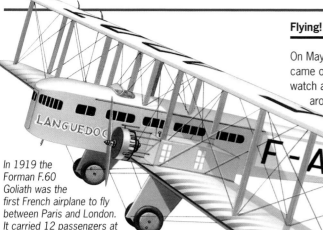

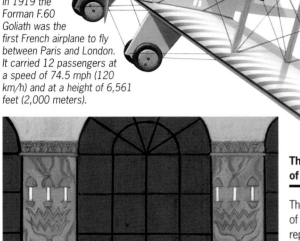

In 1919 the Forman F.60 Goliath was the first French airplane to fly between Paris and London. It carried 12 passengers at a speed of 74.5 mph (120 km/h) and at a height of 6,561 feet (2,000 meters).

Flying!

On May 20, 1927, Parisians came out into the streets to watch an airplane circle around the Eiffel Tower.

It was *The Spirit of Saint Louis* with its youthful American pilot Charles Lindbergh, who had just completed the first solo flight across the Atlantic Ocean in 33 hours. Flying was no longer just a dream. As early as 1919, airline companies existed, and by the end of the 1920s they connected Paris with most of the great European cities. On board passengers were served champagne and canapés of paté de fois, prepared by Chez Maxim.

The Crisis of 1929

The Wall Street crash of 1929 had grave repercussions for the Paris stock exchange, and led to the collapse of the French economy. Many factories closed, while the unemployed invaded Paris in search of occasional or temporary work. Reception centers were opened in the suburbs, along with soup kitchens which were administered by the town council and church groups. The crisis was especially hard on women, who had only just begun to enter the workforce as typists, telephone operators, and office clerks.

Art Capital

After World War I, artistic talent bloomed in Paris. Along with French painters like Matisse, there were refugees from central Europe, Spain, Russia, and Italy. Montmarte was abandoned in favor of Montparnasse, which offered bigger and cheaper studios. One of the first painters to move there was Picasso. A bohemian area, it also attracted artists such as Modigliani, Léger, Lipchitz, Brancusi, and Soutine, who could be found sitting in the cafés of La Coupole or Le Dôme in search of patrons. In all artistic fields, the desire for something new produced stars: Schönberg and Alban Berg in music for example, Paul Eluard and André Breton in poetry, and Apollinaire, Proust, Joyce, and Céline in literature.

Matisse's 1924 odalisque in red trousers.

A 1943 French poster condemns the black market (below) while ration books were issued to buy basic items.

Objects on Show

In spring 1925, an international exhibition of Art Déco was held. Here young interior designers, architects, painters, cabinet-makers, tailors, and upholsterers presented their work. They used luxurious materials such as exotic wood, skins, marble, chrome, toughened glass, and mother-of-pearl. The objects they created were often unique pieces or part of a limited series that only a small élite could

The wealthy elite passed their evenings in nightclubs across the city, as depicted in this 1920s print.

afford. Modern artists, such as Le Corbusier, Chareau, and Jourdain, were united against this elitism in their belief that their objects should be available to everyone.

Designed by Gabriel Argy-Rousseau, this glass liqueur service is a fine example of the many Art Deco style objects made in Paris during the 1920s and 1930s.

The economic crisis quickly spread around the world and reached Paris in 1929.

The Nazi Occupation

On September 3, 1939, war was declared on Nazi Germany. The following June Hitler's troops marched down the Champs-Élysées and the city was occupied. The Nazis set up their headquarters in the Luxembourg Palace. The city was not badly damaged during the war, but no buses, taxis, or cars were allowed to run, and the Métro was closed for several hours each day. Many delux restaurants and cabarets stayed open to cater to the occupiers. The French Resistance was active in the city throughout the war and on August 19, 1944 the Communist-led Resistance rose up against the Germans. By that time American troops were close to the city and after just a few days of ferocious street battles, on August 25, Paris was free.

Hardship in World War II

During the German occupation, Paris experienced severe shortages in food, fuel, and all basic necessities. In September 1940, a rationing system was introduced, but the black market still prospered in the city.

1945 – PRESENT

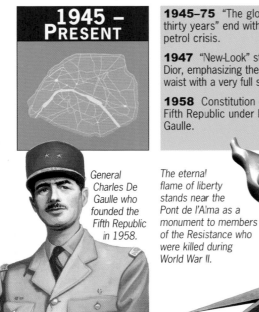

1945–75 "The glorious thirty years" end with the petrol crisis.

1947 "New-Look" style of Dior, emphasizing the small waist with a very full skirt.

1958 Constitution of the Fifth Republic under De Gaulle.

1959–69 André Malraux becomes Minister of Culture and begins work on the restoration of old Paris. He transforms the metro station of the Louvre into an antiquarian museum and launches the idea of "themed" stations.

1968 Student uprisings.

1969 The RER is created. Les Halles is transferred to Rungis.

1973 The polytechnic opens to students.

1975 The first G7 Summit is organized by Valéry Giscard d'Estaing. A statute is passed allowing Parisian councillors to elect a mayor. This gave Paris the same political autonomy as other French towns.

1977 Jacques Chirac is elected first mayor of Paris.

1980 Hundreds of thousands of people greet the Pope, John Paul II, when he visits Paris.

General Charles De Gaulle who founded the Fifth Republic in 1958.

The eternal flame of liberty stands near the Pont de l'Alma as a monument to members of the Resistance who were killed during World War II.

Saint-Germain-des-Prés in the 1950s

After the Liberation, the city's youth, looking for a place to meet, make friends, and exchange ideas, congregated in the quarter of Saint-Germain-des-Prés. It was here that the existentialists, led by Jean-Paul Sartre and Albert Camus, lived and worked. An intellectual élite and artists from all over the world met in cafés like the Flore, where existentialist artists such as Juliette Gréco sang about the soul of Paris. In the quarter's many small theaters experimental plays by young authors were performed. Low-cost movies were made with extensive use of street scenes and the Nouvelle-Vague (New Wave) was launched.

Parisians and tourists relax at the Café de Flore in Saint-Germain-des-Prés.

Above: A poster from May 1968. It reads 'the fight continues'.

1945 to the Present

In the ten years following World War II the French economy was weighed down by the cost of reconstruction. But by the mid-50s, the capital had begun to renew its infrastructure, restoring old quarters such as the Marais, and greatly developing its transportation network. The last 25 years of the 20th century saw enormous public works carried out, and Paris entered the third millenium as a world capital, notable for its fascinating mixture of carefully preserved and restored monuments and buildings, and some thoroughly modern, often audacious, architecture.

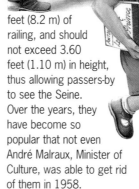

Modern art and haute couture combine. The Yves Saint Laurent collection of 1965 was inspired by the painter Mondrian.

Picasso

The Spanish artist Pablo Picasso lived almost all his artistic life in France. When he died in 1973, the French government accepted many of his works of art in exchange for payment of the heavy death duties which had fallen on his family. Since a home was needed for these works, the Picasso Museum was opened, not in Montparnasse or Montmartre where the artist was most at home, but in the Hôtel Salé in the bourgeois area of the Marais. The collection covers entire periods of Picasso's life, from the red period, to the blue period, to cubism.

A Library by the Seine

Along both embankments of the Seine, the stalls of second-hand booksellers (above) stretch for 2.4 miles (4 km). Offering everything from cartoons to mystery stories, best-sellers to pocket-size books, the city of Paris each year gives out 245 renewable licenses to booksellers. Each stall can occupy a maximum of 26.9 feet (8.2 m) of railing, and should not exceed 3.60 feet (1.10 m) in height, thus allowing passers-by to see the Seine. Over the years, they have become so popular that not even André Malraux, Minister of Culture, was able to get rid of them in 1958.

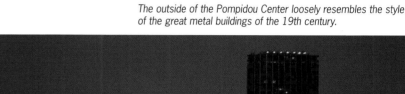

The outside of the Pompidou Center loosely resembles the style of the great metal buildings of the 19th century.

May 1968 — Students on the Streets

During the 1960s, there was rising dissatisfaction with consumer society among the French youth. This discontent was transformed into various student movements, which in Paris were mobilized in the new university buildings at Nanterre. As the police intervened, students at the Sorbonne and high schools around Paris also became involved. There were many violent battles between the police and students, above all in the Latin Quarter. As sympathy developed among the Parisian population at large, these protests moved into the world of work.

The Giant Toy

An international competition to design a new cultural center in Paris was launched by President Georges Pompidou in 1971. The winning design was conceived by the architects Richard Rogers and Renzo Piano, and was opened by Pompidou's successor, Valérie Giscard d'Estaing in 1977. The world famous Pompidou Center is a work of art in itself, but in complete contrast to the architecture of the surrounding area. Escalators encased in glass tubes, ventilation pipes, transparent lifts, and metal columns dominate the exterior of the 136 feet (42 m) high building. The size of an enormous department store, the center has been described as an "activity container" and attracts tourists and Parisians alike. One of the many cultural and artistic institutions housed inside, the National Museum of Modern Art displays the work of artists such as Matisse, Miró, Picasso, Chagall, and Pollock.

Not only the Métro

The transport system RER (urban railway) serves commuter traffic and travels in tunnels in the center and suburbs of Paris. Curiously each train has a name, such as Alex or Vera, which helps to identify it.

RER stations are indicated by these round logos.

RER

Immigration

France, and in particular Paris, has experienced a large amount of immigration over the years. Until the 1980s most immigrants were from other European countries, but now Paris houses thousands of people from Asia, Africa, and eastern Europe too.

A night view of the Monparnasse Tower.

The Montparnasse Tower

A municipal law of 1902 fixed the height of buildings at 98.4 feet (30 m) with exceptions up to 121.39 feet (37 m) allowed. Between 1958 and 1974, however, around 350 buildings went over this limit. Among these was the Montparnasse Tower, built in 1973, and the largest office block in Europe. Built of steel and glass, it is 685 feet (209 m) high and set upon 56 cement pillars. Five thousand people work there everyday. In 1995, an intrepid rock-climber climbed it in one hour and 20 minutes, watched by a stunned audience of police.

Les Halles-Forum

The Parisian market, Les Halles (see pages 20–21 and 27), stood on the same site from 1183 until it was demolished in 1960. In its place today is the Forum (left), which stands on 17 acres (7 h) of land with four underground levels that reach 42 feet (13 m) in depth. Filled with shops, restaurants, and bookshops, it is the busiest metro station in the world. The corolla-shaped pavilions on the outside, 39 feet (12 m) higher than the Forum itself, have also made it one of the biggest attractions in Paris.

The Arch of the Défense with the Calder sculpture in the foreground.

The Great Arch

"A window on the world" and "a symbol of hope for the future" was how the Arch of the Défense, inaugurated on June 14, 1989 for the second centenary of the French Revolution, was described. An open cube, 360 feet (110 m) wide (Notre-Dame could stand inside it), it is covered in white marble from Carrara and stands on 12 pilons reaching 98 feet (30 m) below ground. It dominates the end of the long road

MODERN WORKS

1981–92 The great architectural works of President Mitterrand are built.

1987 The IMA (Arab World Institute) is built by Jean Nouvel.

1989 The Louvre Pyramid, the Arch of the Défense, and the Opéra-Bastille are all completed. The Ministry of Finance moves to Bercy. Its new building is conceived as a point of access to the city and features a long bridge-like structure.

from the Arch de Triomphe du Carrousel at the Louvre, and was designed by the Danish architect, Otto von Spreckelsen in response to President Mitterrand's public competition in 1982. Mitterrand set international architects a challenge; he asked them to free their imaginations and rid

themselves of constraints. The result was von Spreckelsen's magnificent arch.

Below: The Grand Louvre is approached through a glass Pyramid which illuminates the main entrance to the museum (the Hall Napoléon). From inside visitors can admire the old parts of the building.

Paris Renews Itself

The Opera-Bastille

President Mitterrand also commissioned a new Opera House to stand on the site of the old Bastille station. In 1983, the young Canadian architect Carlos Ott was awarded the project. His choice of building materials sought to combine modernity (glass and steel), with tradition (stone). Semi-circular in shape, the building is 164 feet (50 m) high, and accessed by a monumental staircase. Despite its enormous size, the Opéra Bastille (left) was artfully conceived to harmonize with the much smaller surrounding buildings.

In the 1980s, President François Mitterrand embarked upon a series of *grands projets* ("great projects") that would change the face of Paris and involve architects from around the world. Major projects included the Louvre Pyramid, the transformation of the old Gare d'Orsay into a museum (Musee d'Orsay), and the development of the Défense area on the outskirts of the city. The overall scope of the projects was huge and by the late 1980s an estimated 2,000 architectural teams world-wide were working on Parisian projects. Alongside the stunning new modernistic buildings and monuments, some olders areas, such as the picturesque Sainte-Geneviève district in the Latin Quarter, were carefully renovated.

Open-Air Sculpture

The futuristic landscape of the Défense is made friendlier by a series of open-air sculptures. These include Calder's *Stabile* and

Miró's fantasy sculpture. At Beaubourg, there is the Nikki de Saint-Phalle and Jean Tinguely Fountain (above), made of multicolored moving parts.

Disneyland Paris

Disneyland Paris lies in Marne-la-Vallée, some 19.8 miles (32 km) to the east of Paris. Opened in 1992, it covers 4,942 acres (2,000 hectares). Although it maintains the American spirit of Disneyland in Los Angeles with Mickey and Minnie Mouse (left), it retains a European flavor with characters like Peter Pan, Alice in Wonderland,

and the Sleeping Beauty. It is visited by thousands of tourists, both children and adults, every year.

1990 The CNIT (National Center for Industry and Technology) is reorganized with hotels, restaurants, commercial buildings, and a golf course.

1990–2015 Programme of resettlement in Paris and the Île de France, as entire quarters are remodeled.

1991 The Seine riverbanks are classified as World Heritage Sites by UNESCO.

1993 The Grand Palais hosts the International Fair of Contemporary Art (FIAC).

1996 The National Library of France opens near Austerlitz station. Constructed of four towers, each in the form of a book, it houses 12 million works and publications. Saint-Honoré shopping and business center opens.

1998 The European Stadium of Saint-Denis is opened.

2001 The EDF Tower, 541 feet (165 m) high, is built at La Défense.

2002 Construction of the CBX Tower, another unusually tall building, begins.

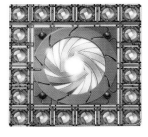

One of the many stunning windows of the glass and steel building that houses the Arab World Institute in Paris.

The Grand Louvre

One of the most important museums in the world, the Louvre Museum had never found enough space in the old palace for its everyday needs. In 1981, President Mitterrand, in one of his first initiatives in office, established the Grand Louvre project. He entrusted the work to the American architect, Ieoh Ming Pei. With orders to respect the original palace and its magnificent architecture, Ieoh Ming Pei was left with only one available space in which to work — the Napoleon courtyard. It was here that the stunning glass pyramid was built, and underneath the Louvre's vast art collections were housed.

Index